D1592801

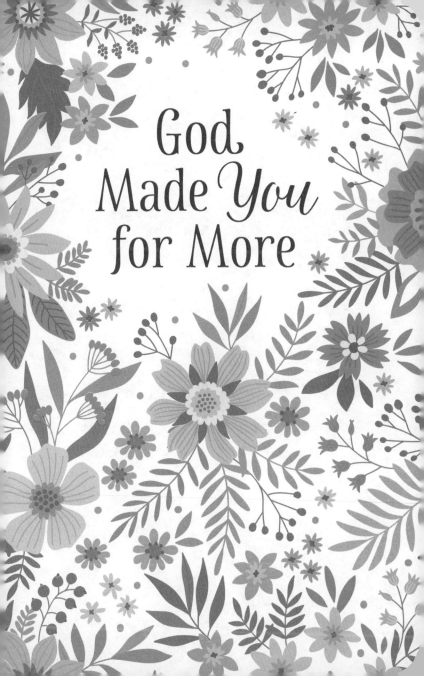

God
Made *You*
for More

God Made You for More

Devotions and Prayers for Women

JANICE THOMPSON

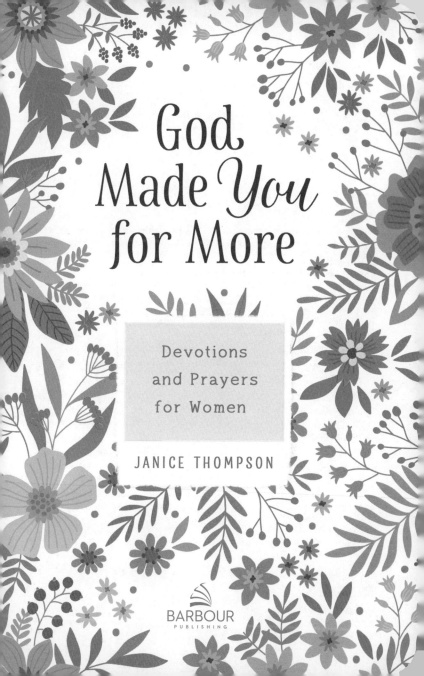

BARBOUR
PUBLISHING

Cover Design: Greg Jackson, Thinkpen Design

Published by Barbour Publishing, Inc., 1810 Barbour Drive, Uhrichsville, Ohio 44683, www.barbourbooks.com

Our mission is to inspire the world with the life-changing message of the Bible.

Member of the
Evangelical Christian
Publishers Association

Printed in China.

God Made You for More

If you've ever watched a made-for-television Charlie Brown program, you probably remember the teacher's voice droning on in the background during the classroom scenes. "Wa-wa. . .wa-wa-wa-wa-wa-wa." Blah, blah, blah. That's how Charlie interpreted his learning experiences. And that's how we often react to our learning experiences too. Life gives us plenty of opportunities to grow, to change—and we roll our eyes and say, "Here we go again!"

God didn't create you to live a boring life. Oh sure, you have a pretty ordinary daily routine (most of us do). You wake up, take care of the kids and get them on the school bus (if you have children at home), head off to work, and so on. Your life feels fairly routine. But in the middle of it all, God wants you to experience micro-adventures. They're waiting for you on the subway as you head off to work; they greet you in the face of a coworker or friend who challenges you to be a better person; they dance around you as you deal with family problems or financial issues.

Whether you're battling through a season of bitterness, heartache, disappointment, fear, insecurity, regret, shame, or unforgiveness, these two hundred comforting, encouraging devotional readings will remind you that you were made for so much more. Each reading, complemented by an uplifting scripture selection and prayer, promises to renew and refresh your spirit with this timeless biblical truth: life in Christ was never meant to be mundane. It can be exciting, refreshing, adventurous, and challenging. (Definitely challenging!) If you keep a positive, upbeat perspective, you'll see that skies are a dizzying shade of blue, clouds roll overhead in puffy imaginative shapes, and children laugh with joy that rivals a glorious sunrise.

God made you for more, sister. Now go and live out His amazing plan for your life!

Yearning for More

"But seek first the kingdom of God and his righteousness, and all these things will be added to you."

MATTHEW 6:33 ESV

"There's got to be more to life than this."

Nadia stared at the pile of bills on the counter and groaned. Life had to be more than coming and going from work, ripping open envelopes stuffed with bills, and dealing with frantic calls from a boss who probably wouldn't even know she existed if not for her expertise at work. It had to be more than kids who argued, a spouse who was always worn out, and friends who were too busy for a cup of coffee.

Surely there *had* to be more.

Right?

Maybe you're like Nadia. You consider your humdrum life and cry out, "Lord, didn't You promise me more? Doesn't Your Word say that I can tread on serpents, move mountains, and impact my generation for You?"

Precious woman, *yes*, you were made for so much more. That's why you're yearning for things you've not yet seen. Don't give up. God has something wonderful planned for you. It's coming. Can you feel it?

Lord, I trust You with the "more" that's coming.
I'll trust and wait on You until I experience it. Amen.

More Life in Your Life

Jesus said to him, "I am the way, and the truth, and the life.
No one comes to the Father except through me."
JOHN 14:6 ESV

Are you one of those people who drags through each day, barely making it through? Or are you someone who has *life* in your life? Do you have a spring in your step, joy in your voice, peace in your countenance? Do you radiate the love and compassion of God to everyone you meet?

It's one thing to live; it's another thing to *completely* offer your life to God in service—giving every moment of every day to Him.

If you're wanting to know how to get more life in your life, it's easy! Real life comes through Jesus Christ. An encounter with the King of kings can (and will!) change everything. Jesus said, "I am the way, and the truth, and the life. No one comes to the Father except through me." It's *only* through Jesus—not through earthly friendships (though those are nice), money (though that's pretty nice too), or even fame that we come to God. The only life worth living is the one He offers.

Father, I'm so grateful You sent Your Son, Jesus,
to bring eternal life. You gave more "life" to my life
when Jesus entered my heart. Thank You! Amen.

More Like Him

Then God said, "Let us make man in our image, after our
likeness. And let them have dominion over the fish of the sea
and over the birds of the heavens and over the livestock and over
all the earth and over every creeping thing that creeps on the
earth." So God created man in his own image, in the image
of God he created him; male and female he created them.

GENESIS 1:26–27 ESV

Remember how as a kid you used to stare at two nearly identical pictures, side by side, and try to spot the differences? You had to stare for a long time to see that one was truly different from the other, but after a while you started to notice the places where one was unique.

Did you know that You were made to look so much like your Creator that people should have to squint and stare to find any differences? It's true! The way you love, the way you speak to others, the way you manage your financial affairs—each of these things (and more!) should be a solid reflection of Him.

Does this mean that God expects you to be perfect? No way! But keep on reflecting Him, sister, and you'll draw people to the One who is truly perfect.

Lord, I want people to see You in me. Make me
more like You every day—in every way. Amen.

More Hope for the Future

There is surely a future hope for you,
and your hope will not be cut off.

PROVERBS 23:18 NIV

Women of purpose know they're made for more, and that includes more hope for the future. Sure, the vast unknown can be scary, especially when you can't see what's coming around the bend.

But while others around you might be cowering in fear as life throws sour pickles their way, you can lift your head high. Things might get tough (sure!), but you won't give up. You have hope—not just for the situations you're facing today, but for tomorrow as well.

You're anticipating great things from the Lord (even though your current circumstances might be arguing to the contrary). Does this mean you will be bowled over if troubles come your way? Nope. You'll take them in stride, because that's what women of hope do. They learn their lessons, square their shoulders, and keep moving forward—one day (and one foot!) at a time.

Lord, I'm a woman of hope. I know You designed me
this way. I place my trust, my hope, and all my
tomorrows in Your hands, Father. Amen.

More Time with God

Draw near to God, and he will draw near to you.
Cleanse your hands, you sinners, and purify
your hearts, you double-minded.

JAMES 4:8 ESV

The clock ticks away the minutes, and you're blissfully unaware of how fast the hands of time are moving. One day you have a tiny baby boy; the next he's a teen learning to drive. One minute you're a young bride; the next you're welcoming your third grandchild.

Time is both friend and foe, isn't it? And though we usually find the hours for spending time with family or friends, we don't always pay the same consideration to the Lord. When it comes to our prayer and Bible reading time, we squeeze the minutes like penny-pinchers. We say things like, "I'm so busy" or "You just don't understand."

But God *does* understand. He knows you're busy. He also knows the importance of not being stingy when it comes to your quiet time, because that's where you find your strength. You were made to spend more time with your Creator; He longs for it and wants you to desire the same. So, make the time, sister. You'll come away stronger for it.

Father, I long to spend more time with You.
I'm honored to be in Your presence. Amen.

More Than Your Pain

For I consider that the sufferings of this present time are not worth comparing with the glory that is to be revealed to us.

ROMANS 8:18 ESV

Marla groaned as she rolled over in bed. For months agonizing joint pain kept her in constant agony. She tried everything the doctors suggested—over the counter pain relievers, prescriptions, massage therapy, and even a chiropractor. Nothing seemed to ease the ongoing pain. On days like this, when she struggled to do even the smallest tasks, Marla wondered if she would ever be more than her pain.

Perhaps you're walking through a similar season. The pain grips like a vise and whispers in your ear, *You're mine. I'm holding you captive! You'll never escape me.*

Here's the good news about your pain: God is bigger. He's bigger than your diagnosis. He's bigger than the prescriptions. He's bigger than the situation. And He loves you—*bigger.* His love for you supersedes the agony you're facing in this moment.

He's *more than* your pain. And He wants to ease your burdens—physical and emotional. Don't give in to defeat. Don't listen to the voice of the enemy as he whispers, *Normal life is behind you.* It's not. God is waiting to prove that to you, so don't give up.

Lord, I give my pain and discomfort to You.
My trust is in You, Jesus. Amen.

More Than Your Past

Listen to me, O royal daughter; take to heart what I say.
Forget your people and your family far away.
Psalm 45:10 nlt

Some people wear their past mistakes like a cloak of shame. They tug it on before walking out the door, despite the fact that it no longer fits. Weeks, months, or years may have passed, but they're still stuck in that coat, as if God had never forgiven them.

You're *not* a product, a victim, or a shameful example of your past. Your past doesn't define you; it doesn't hold a sign over your head that reads: "Listen, everyone! This woman right here used to be a total loser! What a mess! Just ask me, and I'll tell you!"

Aren't you glad your past isn't able to make such a terrible (and public!) proclamation about who you used to be? You're not that woman anymore. You were made for so much more than your past. It's over—done with. Never to be thrown in your face again. God has forgiven you and set you free. The cloak of freedom is the only one you need to wear from here on out—and it fits you beautifully.

Hallelujah!

Father, I'm so glad You've forgiven me for the sins of yesterday.
Thank You for an amazing today and a hopeful tomorrow. Amen.

More Than Your Problems

God is our refuge and strength,
always ready to help in times of trouble.
PSALM 46:1 NLT

Pick up the kids from school. *Check.*

Pay the water bill before the water gets shut off. *Check.*

Deal with the squabble going on between best friends. *Check.*

Figure out why the AC is on the fritz again. *Check.*

Pay for new AC. *Ugh!*

Juggle checkbook to accommodate payment for new AC. *Hmm.*

Life seems to be a series of problems, doesn't it? Sometimes they hit one after the other. You barely catch your breath after one fiasco before another pops up. Problem-solving becomes like a game of whack-a-mole. You can't keep up.

But know this: you are so much more than your problems. Yes, you're in a rough season. Ain't no denying that, sister! But it *will* come to an end; you'll get through it. Then you'll put your feet up, rest against the pillows, and thank the Lord for seeing you through all of it. Just trust. It's going to happen.

I trust You, Lord. I know I was created for more than
my problems. You're in control, Father. Amen.

More Than Your Enemies

*"But to you who are listening I say: Love your enemies,
do good to those who hate you, bless those who
curse you, pray for those who mistreat you."*
LUKE 6:27–28 NIV

Sharla groaned as her "friend" Missy drove by. The woman could keep on driving, as far as she was concerned. After hearing that Missy had tried to make a move on Sharla's husband, Sharla was livid. Missy had better keep her hands—and her charms—to herself, thank you very much. And if she ever came close enough, Sharla would say so to her face.

Not that Sharla's husband, Dave, seemed to notice Missy's advances. He only had eyes for Sharla and always would. Still, that didn't stop Missy from trying.

Maybe you've had an enemy like this—one who would do *anything* to hurt you. It's hard to know what to do with these people, isn't it? If you were in Sharla's position, you would probably want to knock Missy upside her head—but that's not God's way. God is not asking you to be best friends, but you can still pray for the one who wronged you.

Forgiving someone in a situation like Sharla's will likely be one of the hardest things you'll ever do; but if you go ahead and forgive, it will save you years of bitterness and grief.

*Okay, Lord. I'll do it. I'll pray for the one
who has hurt me. Here goes, Lord....*

More with God on Your Side

*"[May] all this assembly. . .know that the LORD saves
not with sword and spear. For the battle is the LORD's,
and he will give you into our hand."*

1 SAMUEL 17:47 ESV

As a teen, Paula enjoyed a game of volleyball as well as the next girl,
but she wasn't the best at the game. Oh, she gave it her best but could
barely get the ball over the net—even on a good day.

Paula especially loved it when her older sister, Arlene, decided
to play. Wow, she was good! With Arlene on the team, they won every
single game. Arlene brought star power to the court. She awed folks
on both sides of the net, and there was never any question about who
would come out a victor.

That's what it's like when you realize God is on your side. He has
superb skills that no human being has. Spectators all through the gym
cheer when the God of the universe takes His turn at serving the ball.
Whoosh! He takes care of things in a hurry, doesn't He?

*God, I'm so glad You're on my side. You have my back even
when others don't. And. . .wow! You even "wow" my enemies,
Father. I'm grateful for Your intervention. Amen.*

More Than Your Disappointments

Do not be anxious about anything, but in everything by prayer and supplication with thanksgiving let your requests be made known to God. And the peace of God, which surpasses all understanding, will guard your hearts and your minds in Christ Jesus.

PHILIPPIANS 4:6–7 ESV

You waited for ages and finally received your answer. But unfortunately, it's not the one you were hoping for. You didn't get the loan for the new house. You're disappointed, as anyone would be. Your mind is troubled, and you can't seem to figure out why things happened this way. More than anything, you're grieved by the loss of what could have been.

Now what should you do? Where do you go with that broken heart of yours? Do you give up altogether or try to get a loan for a different house?

Disappointments come no matter how much you wish them away. But you can take those disappointments to your heavenly Father and ask for His perspective. Perhaps He has a better house waiting for you at a lower price. Or maybe the house you had your eyes on wasn't the right school district for your children—and God knows what they need. Ultimately, He has a terrific plan for you, and you can trust Him with the details.

Lord, I don't understand, but I do choose to trust. I'm more than my disappointments, Father. Thank You for bringing hope to every situation. Amen.

More Than Your Fear

I sought the LORD, and he answered me
and delivered me from all my fears.
PSALM 34:4 ESV

As a little girl, Melanie struggled to fall asleep because she was afraid of the ghosts under her bed. No one could convince her that they weren't there. As she grew, so did her fears. And by the time she reached her teen years, she had irrational fears about diseases, strangers, and many other things.

When she got married, Melanie was terrified her husband would leave her. She lashed out at him—her fears triggering her insecurities—and one day her fears became a self-fulfilling prophecy. Her husband gave up and left.

It took a lot of time and counseling for Melanie to come to grips with the fact that fear was quickly undoing her life. With the help of a Christian therapist, she came to understand this truth: there's no fear in love. God truly can—and *will*—cast out fear if you let Him.

Maybe you're like Melanie, and fear has been ruling your life. If so, it's time to kick it to the curb. You have nothing to fear; you were created for better things.

Lord, I refuse to give in to fear. Thank You for the
reminder that I was made for more! Amen.

More Than Your Insecurity

*"Fear not, therefore; you are of more
value than many sparrows."*

MATTHEW 10:31 ESV

"They don't like me."

"I look awful."

"Why can't I ever get my act together like all of the other women I know?"

"Why am I so fat? Ugh!"

Maybe you've been known to speak a few of these lines to yourself. When you're insecure, doubts can easily plague you—especially if the people in your circle are going out of their way to make you feel "less than."

But God made you to be more than your insecurities and doubts. You are truly of more value than many sparrows, just as God's Word says. He created you in His image, His precious child, beautiful in His sight.

Oh, I know. You read those words and cringe. How could anyone—*even God*—call you beautiful? And yet He does. He sees no flaws when He looks at you. He sees a delightful, charming girl, bone of His bone and flesh of His flesh. And He wants nothing more than to convince you that you're worthy of His amazing love.

*Lord, Your love for me is beyond all I could imagine. Thank You
for finding value in me. I feel so loved by You, Jesus. Amen.*

More Than Your Regrets

*If we confess our sins, he is faithful and just to forgive us
our sins and to cleanse us from all unrighteousness.*

1 JOHN 1:9 ESV

If she could have changed it, she would have. Brenda winced every time she remembered how she'd spoken to her best friend on the day of "the big falling out," as she'd taken to calling it. Gloria hadn't spoken to her since that terrible day, and Brenda really couldn't blame her. Who blew up like that and said such cruel things to a good friend? *Ugh.* Could she ever make things right between them? Or would things always be just as they were right now—tense and ugly?

Maybe you've blown up in the same way. You've spoken to a parent, a child, a spouse, a friend, or a coworker in a way that you regret. It was out of character for you, but now everyone sees you as some sort of horrible person to be avoided.

God can take a situation—even one as difficult as yours—and mend it. Extend a hand of apology. Speak the twelve words that can heal a relationship: "I am sorry. I was wrong. Please forgive me. I love you." Then watch as God makes your regrets a thing of the past.

*Lord, I don't know how You can fix the situations
that seem beyond repair, but I place them
in Your hands today. Amen.*

More Than Your Unforgiveness

"If you forgive others their trespasses, your heavenly Father will also forgive you, but if you do not forgive others their trespasses, neither will your Father forgive your trespasses."
MATTHEW 6:14-15 ESV

You've tried to forgive. You've paced the floor, begging God to help you let it go. You've written letters to release the person from the pain they've caused, but then you didn't mail them. A part of you wants to cling to hurt; it has become a part of you, and you're reluctant to let go. Yet it's eating you alive.

If only. . .

You were made to forgive. It's that simple (and that difficult). God forgives you and expects you to forgive others. Have you been badly hurt? Yes. Is that person apologetic or even remorseful? Probably not. Does that mean you have the satisfaction of holding him (or her) in unforgiveness forever?

No.

And. . .no.

You *have* to forgive. It's not a suggestion; it's a mandate that will save your life because it will release you from the demons of bitterness. When this happens, the one who is set free is not your adversary—it's you.

Lord, today I choose to forgive the one who has hurt me, once and for all. Show me how, I pray. Amen.

21

More Than Your Bitterness

*Be angry and do not sin; do not let the sun go down
on your anger, and give no opportunity to the devil.*
EPHESIANS 4:26–27 ESV

She always looks like she's been sucking on lemons, Janie thought to herself as she glanced across the church at an older woman named Cora.

Anyone who knew Cora very well knew the truth: Cora was overflowing with bitterness that dated back to the breakup of her marriage twenty years ago. She still couldn't get past the pain her ex-husband had caused. She stewed every time his name came up in conversation. The bitterness had settled deep in her heart and created the same effect one might expect if they added a slow-acting poison to a perfectly lovely chocolate cake. Over time, it was killing her.

And everyone noticed, but no one said anything. Janie wondered if Cora would ever release her ex and truly forgive him. If she would do that, everything could change in an instant. Should she bring it up in conversation?

Perhaps you've been in Janie's shoes, with a friend drowning in the deep waters of bitterness. Or maybe you're the one who has had trouble letting go. It's time to realize, as God's girls, we are so much more than our bitterness!

Lord, may I never let the sun go down on my anger. Amen.

More Than Your Shame

Instead of your shame there shall be a double portion; instead of dishonor they shall rejoice in their lot; therefore in their land they shall possess a double portion; they shall have everlasting joy.

ISAIAH 61:7 ESV

She wore the shame like a shroud. It served as a filter to every decision she made in life—a barrier to every friendship, a barricade to any potential successes. If she could go back and change the past, she would; but Carrigan would never have the chance to make right what she had done wrong. One terrible decision as a teen had resulted in overwhelming guilt she just couldn't shake.

"You have to get past this, Carrigan," everyone said. "God has forgiven you. You need to forgive yourself." But every time she would think about releasing herself from the guilt, the shame—those old feelings—would wash back over her yet again.

God created us for so much more than our shame. Countless scriptures prove a very good point: the Lord doesn't want us to live in the past, and that shroud of shame you've been wearing is a garment from yesterday.

Forgive yourself. Whether your mistake was an accident or on purpose. No matter the consequences. No matter *who* or *what* or *where* or *when*. Allow God to wash you clean once and for all.

Lord, today is the day I once and for all let go of the shame I've clung to. Amen.

More Than Your Suffering

We can rejoice, too, when we run into problems and trials, for we know that they help us develop endurance. And endurance develops strength of character, and character strengthens our confident hope of salvation.

ROMANS 5:3–4 NLT

Irma went through many struggles in her young life. She battled systemic lupus and was hospitalized several times with kidney failure. Her suffering seemed endless. As she got into her thirties and forties, sickness was her constant companion. Before long she became known as "Oh, Irma? The one with lupus?" She hated that description but understood that people didn't mean to label her.

Maybe you've been labeled because of your suffering too. You're "Jessica, the one going through chemo," or "Mary, the lady in the wheelchair." You're tired of the labels but don't know how to get past them.

You were made for more than your suffering, sister—whether physical or emotional. No matter what label the world sticks on you, God calls you His precious daughter. So cast aside any name that doesn't fit and proclaim to the world, "I'm more than all that!"

You are a daughter of the King!

I am more than my labels, Lord.
And I'm so grateful You see me as Yours. Amen.

More Than Rejected

No, God has not rejected his own people,
whom he chose from the very beginning.
ROMANS 11:2 NLT

It didn't make any sense. She and Lizzy were best friends. Why would her bestie host a party, invite so many others, but exclude her? Marla couldn't understand what had happened. Sure, the ladies on the invitation list were all part of a larger clique at work. That much she knew. But Lizzy had never been part of that clique—at least not to Marla's knowledge.

Familiar feelings crept over Marla; she had known the sting of rejection from her teen years. The boyfriend who claimed he'd always love her had dumped her. The deadbeat dad who rarely came around but one day showed up—wanting money. And now this?

Maybe you've walked a mile in Marla's shoes. You've felt the ache of rejection from someone you thought was a friend. Or maybe a group of women at church hasn't opened their arms to you just yet—they're far too busy laughing and chatting with each other even to notice you've walked in the door.

Today, know and trust that God will *never* reject you. You're His precious child, and He created you to be included—by Him *and* His people.

Lord, today I give You my feelings of rejection.
Thank You for always including me, Father! Amen.

More Than Cast Aside

*As you come to him, a living stone rejected by men
but in the sight of God chosen and precious.*
1 PETER 2:4 ESV

Kennedy struggled with feelings of abandonment and rejection from early childhood through adulthood. Being adopted by a loving family wasn't enough to ease the pain of rejection she felt. Why had her mother given her up in the first place? Was she too much of a burden? What were the circumstances?

When Kennedy grew up, she married a wonderful man and had four beautiful children, but she still never got over those burdensome feelings of being unwanted. She deliberately pushed her husband and children away, convinced they didn't really want her. It took the intervention of family members and the help of a great Christian therapist for Kennedy to come to grips with the truth—she was more than her feelings of rejection.

Perhaps you've been rejected too. You've been cast aside by a parent, a spouse, a group of friends. You're struggling with the "whys" of it all. Beautiful woman, God will *never* abandon you. You're His—forever. In His sight, you are chosen and precious *always.*

*Lord, thank You for seeing me as precious! I know You'll never reject
me, Father. This knowledge brings great joy to my heart. Amen.*

More Than Broken

"I have told you all this so that you may have peace in me.
Here on earth you will have many trials and sorrows.
But take heart, because I have overcome the world."
JOHN 16:33 NLT

Reena gasped aloud as the delicate vase hit the floor. Water splashed everything in sight, and the gorgeous daffodils went tumbling out onto the floor. She wasn't worried about either of those things; only the broken vase concerned her. A gift from her aunt in Italy, it was Reena's prized possession. And now it was shattered to pieces.

While you can often glue a broken vase back together again, what do you do with a broken life? Maybe you've been like that vase—tragically shattered into a thousand little pieces. You didn't cause the situation; you had no control over it. But still the pieces lay scattered all over the floor.

Only God can put together what has been broken in your life. Do you trust Him? Today is a wonderful day to acknowledge that you were made for more than brokenness. Let the heavenly Father mend you, that you may be made whole again.

Lord, I give You every broken piece of me.
Do the kind of mending that only You can. Amen.

More Patience

*Love is patient, love is kind. It does not envy, it does not boast,
it is not proud. It does not dishonor others, it is not self-seeking,
it is not easily angered, it keeps no record of wrongs.*

1 CORINTHIANS 13:4–5 NIV

"You were created to be more patient."

Ouch. Perhaps those words cause a twinge of pain in your spirit. You don't want to be more patient, thank you very much. You've been patient enough already—with people, with circumstances, with a never-ending flow of problems. How could the Lord possibly expect you to be even more patient? That hardly seems fair.

But wait. Hasn't He been patient with you? Wasn't He right there loving you even when you turned your back on Him and tried to walk away? God wants you to learn from His example—to experience (and convey) that sort of patience with all the people you come in contact with.

Yes, even the ones you struggle with.

Especially the ones you struggle with.

*Lord, having patience doesn't come naturally to me. But I know
that I can do it with Your help. Show me how to exhibit more
patience so that I can be more like You, Father. Amen.*

More Time in Passionate Response

"But ask the beasts, and they will teach you; the birds of the heavens, and they will tell you; or the bushes of the earth, and they will teach you; and the fish of the sea will declare to you. Who among all these does not know that the hand of the LORD has done this? In his hand is the life of every living thing and the breath of all mankind."

JOB 12:7–10 ESV

What does it mean to respond with passion to the Lord? Every day miracles are happening around you. The sun rises in the morning and sets in the evening in brilliant Technicolor display. Babies are born; trees sprout leaves; flowers push up from the ground. All of this happens with just a word from our gracious heavenly Father. And how do we respond to it all? Mostly we take it for granted. Every now and again we're captivated by snowcapped mountains or a baby's soft cheeks. We respond with a passionate, heartfelt "Wow!"

It's time to respond to the heavenly Creator's daily miracles with the awe they deserve! Look out the window. Nature beckons you to respond in adoration to the Master Creator.

Lord, You made it all! Those brilliant colors. Those magnificent views. Every bright and glorious thing was created by and for You. Thank You for sharing your artistry with mankind, Father! Amen.

More of Him, Less of You

Incline my heart to your testimonies,
and not to selfish gain!
PSALM 119:36 ESV

Commercials tout it, Hollywood insists upon it, even schools teach it: self comes first. Whatever self wants, self gets. Whatever self craves, self shall have.

This is the opposite of what God's Word says, of course! To have more of Him, we need to desire less of ourselves.

What does this look like in the real world? Less of you, more of Him means you have to sacrifice the flesh when you're wanting to sleep in instead of going to the Bible study you promised you'd attend. It means you have to swallow hard and not bite back when someone snaps at you.

Saying no to the flesh means caring more about others than yourself. (Need an example? Remember when you were a kid and your mama made fried chicken and you always insisted on the thigh piece? It's time to let that go now. Give that thigh to someone else, girl. You take the leg. It's just as tasty.)

Less of you. It's not always easy, but it's always right if you want more of Him.

Today I offer You all of me, Lord—that I might
die to self and live to worship You. Amen.

More Acknowledgment of What Christ Did

For the word of the cross is folly to those who are perishing, but to us who are being saved it is the power of God.

1 CORINTHIANS 1:18 ESV

Bridgette came to know the Lord as a youngster. She gave her heart totally and fully to Him, accepting Jesus as Savior and King of her heart. From that moment on, she did her best to live a life worthy of her calling.

Over time she got involved in several church projects. As a young mom, she headed up the mother's group. Then she joined the choir and offered to help the director. She stayed busy, busy, busy. If you had said, "Tell me about your faith," she probably would have filled your ears with stories of all the ways she volunteered at her church but little about her faith journey. Truthfully, her faith took a distant second place to her busyness.

Maybe you're in the same boat. You're so tied to your church that it now represents your faith. You can't seem to remember where your salvation leaves off and your church busyness begins.

Maybe it's time to take a breath and examine the two—as two separate entities. You were made to acknowledge what Christ did to transform your life, after all!

Lord, I love my church and enjoy the busyness, but may I never forget the work You've done in my heart! I'm forever grateful. Amen.

More Authenticity

*For our boast is this, the testimony of our conscience,
that we behaved in the world with simplicity and godly
sincerity, not by earthly wisdom but by the grace
of God, and supremely so toward you.*

2 CORINTHIANS 1:12 ESV

"She's such a fake. You can see right through her."

Debbie wished she hadn't overheard her so-called friend's assessment of her, but what could she do about it now? Did her friends really see her as a fake? Was she?

Okay, so she tried a little too hard. And yes, she laughed too loud, tried to be the center of attention whenever possible. But Debbie thought all those things would endear her to people, not turn them away.

Maybe you've been there. You've been accused of not being authentic. Or maybe you have a friend who spends too much time faking it.

God designed you to be authentically you. No one else. Nothing put on. Nothing over-the-top. Just you. So relax. Be yourself. Don't be afraid to let your guard down and allow people to get to know you—the *real* you.

*Lord, I want to be authentic—not just in Your
sight but in the sight of others. I need Your
help to let go of the facade, Father. Amen.*

More in the Lean Seasons

In this you rejoice, though now for a little while,
if necessary, you have been grieved by various trials.
1 PETER 1:6 ESV

In Old Testament times, the people of God went through seasons of plenty and seasons of lack. During seasons of plenty, they celebrated the Lord's goodness. During seasons of lack, they learned to put their trust in Him. Through it all, they also discovered the joy of making provision during the seasons of plenty so that their needs would be met later on.

God never meant for lean seasons to break you. He wants you to be prepared—physically and psychologically—no matter what's going on around you. Wouldn't it be terrific if, during tough times, you were prepared to help others in crisis? How marvelous would it be if your storehouses were full so that they could spill over onto your neighbors in need?

The Lord created you for more—in every season, good and bad. No matter where you are right now, you can trust Him to provide everything you need and more.

Lord, I choose to trust You even in my seasons of lack.
I was made for more than the lean seasons, Father.
Thank You for that reminder. Amen.

More in the Days of Tribulation

*"Now when these things begin to take place,
straighten up and raise your heads, because
your redemption is drawing near."*

LUKE 21:28 ESV

Brittany wasn't ready for catastrophe to hit. The nation was under a quarantine due to a virus, and she had been caught off-guard. Panic gripped her as she watched the news. Fear took hold when she had to go out in public. All around her, neighbors and friends were stockpiling food and other essentials, as if the world were coming to an end. It was almost more than she could take—psychologically or financially.

Perhaps you've reacted like Brittany during a crisis; you wanted to shut off the news and pretend everything was normal. God wants you to be prepared for seasons of tribulation—whether they're national, physical (things like catastrophic illness), or financial (the loss of a job or other financial losses).

You are *more* in the days of tribulation. More faith. More hope. More joy. More kindness to others. More of a blessing to those in need. More dedicated to spreading the Word.

Tribulation will come, and you will soar because of the "more."

*Lord, I must admit, trying seasons are so very difficult.
But I choose to trust You. I was made for more than
tribulation. Thank You for that reminder. Amen.*

More Perfect Love, Less Fear

There is no fear in love. Perfect love puts fear out of our hearts.
People have fear when they are afraid of being punished.
The man who is afraid does not have perfect love.

1 JOHN 4:18 NLV

As a child, you probably dreamed of the perfect love story—for a prince on a white horse to sweep in and carry you off to his magical kingdom where all your collective dreams would come true. You probably didn't count on the fairy tale having bumps in the road—like a job loss or a child born with a chromosomal abnormality. You certainly didn't imagine your story with the repossession of a car or the death of your best friend from cancer.

Here's a hard truth: good times and bad usually reside side by side. Many of the greatest blessings of your life will take place during some of the toughest seasons. And if you keep your focus on God, He can squelch any fears you might experience—even in the deepest valleys.

Where are you now? Is your "happily ever after" being crowded out by pain? Take a deep breath. Ask God to take your fears and channel them into something amazing, something long-lasting. He desires you to stay strong, and that can't happen if fear has you locked in its embrace.

Let go of your fear—right in this very moment.

There. Doesn't that feel better?

I choose to trust You even in the frightening times, Lord. I was made
for more love and less fear. Thank You for this reminder. Amen.

More in the Good Times

Every good gift and every perfect gift is from above,
coming down from the Father of lights, with whom
there is no variation or shadow due to change.
JAMES 1:17 ESV

Have you ever felt guilty when things were going right? Sure, you've had hard seasons. But then a blissful one comes. The bills are paid. The kids are healthy. Your parents are doing well. The neighbors are all getting along. And for whatever reason, you start feeling badly that things are okay in your world. You look around and notice the friend who is going through a divorce, and you're feeling guilty that your marriage is strong and steady. You see that loved one walking down a dark road with cancer, and you feel terrible sharing the news that your latest mammogram came back clean.

God wants you to enjoy the good seasons, sister! Even those people you're fretting over want you to celebrate the blissful times. If they could say anything to you right now, it might be this: "Girl! You think I want you to suffer just because I'm suffering? You think I want you unhappy just because I'm unhappy? Not a chance!"

Pray for those in need. Take care of them. Send cards. Give hugs. Show up. But don't, under any circumstances, sacrifice the joy of where you are today.

Lord, thank You for all of life's seasons—good and bad. Amen.

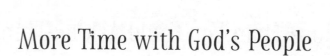

More Time with God's People

Let us consider how to stir up one another to love and good works, not neglecting to meet together, as is the habit of some, but encouraging one another, and all the more as you see the Day drawing near.

HEBREWS 10:24–25 ESV

"I'm so busy." Anita's nose wrinkled as she spoke. "I don't have time to join a Bible study or go to Wednesday evening services at church. I'm so overloaded with work and family that I can barely make it to church on Sunday mornings."

Maybe you can relate to Anita's woes. You're busy too. You have a family, a job, meals to cook, a mortgage to pay. Making the time to spend with other Christians is tough, no matter how hard you try.

Oh, but you need to try, sister! God didn't intend for you to go it alone. The more you hang out with other believers, the stronger you'll become. The Lord designed you to spend more time with His people, after all. So stop with the excuses and get to it! You'll be so glad you did.

I need more time with my church family, Lord!
No more excuses. I'm going to show up and
link arms with those around me. Amen.

More Than You Could Ask or Think

*Now all glory to God, who is able, through his
mighty power at work within us, to accomplish
infinitely more than we might ask or think.*
EPHESIANS 3:20 NLT

"I want a pink pony and a unicorn and some cotton candy!"

As a three-year-old, you wanted it all—didn't you? You wanted sunshine, lollipops, rainbows, great friends, princess parties, snow globes, trips to amusement parks, and every other wonderful thing your imagination could dream of.

You haven't changed much, truth be told. That anticipation of "more than you could ask or think" is straight from heaven. God has promised it to you in His Word. And the reason you feel comfortable asking God for the impossible is because He's known for accomplishing the impossible. Praying for a sick friend? He can handle it. Praying for a financial miracle? He's pretty amazing at that too.

Of course, pink ponies and unicorns might be out of the question—at least for now—but don't be afraid to ask for just about anything else your heart desires.

*I'm so glad You're a God who loves my requests, Lord!
Thank You for providing so many of the things I've asked
for over the years. My gratitude overflows! Amen.*

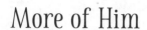

More of Him

I want to know Him. I want to have the same power in my life
that raised Jesus from the dead. I want to understand and have
a share in His sufferings and be like Christ in His death.
Philippians 3:10 nlv

Imagine that someone gives you a puzzle to work, but there's no lid to the box. You don't know what the final picture is supposed to look like. You're only able to piece together one little section at a time, with no understanding of the final product.

In some ways, following the Lord is a lot like that. You know He's good; you're sure He loves You. But you don't see "all" of Him. He's revealing Himself to you in snippets—one tiny puzzle piece at a time. As the segments of the story come into focus, you're more convinced than ever that He's in control and cares for you. But even then you don't have a full understanding.

Isn't it wonderful to know that heaven will provide all the answers you're seeking? And you don't have to wait until then to know God better. His Word says that you can know Him even now—not just in the power of His resurrection, but in the fellowship of His suffering. No matter what you're walking through, He longs to reveal more of Himself to you today.

Lord, I want to know You more. I was created to
be intimately acquainted with You. Amen.

More Spiritual Growth

*Anyone who lives on milk cannot understand the
teaching about being right with God. He is a baby.*
HEBREWS 5:13 NLV

If you've ever watched a baby's growth over the first few years, you understand how dramatically things can change in a very short period of time. One minute he's cooing at his mother's breast; the next he's a tyrannical toddler, knocking plants off the end table. One minute she's dressed in preemie clothes that are still too big; the next minute a size four diaper is too small. Babies grow and grow and grow. You take lots of snapshots because you're afraid you'll forget what each brief stage looked like. My, the days whiz right by!

God wants to see this same kind of growth from you once you give your heart to Him. Like that babe, you need to change sizes as the days, weeks, months, and years go by—no, not physically—He wants you to grow and develop in your faith, to have such a lasting change in attitude, spirit, and demeanor that people can barely remember what you were like before. It's time to stop living on milk, girl, and head for the meat and potatoes of His Word.

*Father, I'm ready to grow up in You. I want to
be all You planned for me to be. Amen.*

More Beauty around You

In the beginning God created the heavens and the earth. Now the earth was formless and empty, darkness was over the surface of the deep, and the Spirit of God was hovering over the waters.

GENESIS 1:1–2 NIV

"Breathtaking!" You stare at the waters of the mighty Pacific, overcome by the sight of the waves striking the cliffs. They pound away with great force and then roll gently back out to sea.

"Amazing!" You marvel at the sight of the Rocky Mountains capped in white frosting in the distance. They take away your breath.

"Unbelievable!" You stare into the bright blue eyes of your best friend's newborn while listening to the baby's gentle coos and gurgles. Magnificent!

All of creation points to its unique Creator, who cared enough to make the skies a brilliant blue and clouds a fluffy white, and to dress penguins in lovely tuxedos. He thought you needed to be pretty special too, so He designed you specifically, just as you are—part of this beautiful creation you're meant to enjoy.

Lord, thank You for creating such a colorful, joyous planet for me to live on. Every day is a feast for the eyes and heart. I'm so grateful. Amen.

More Passionate
Response to the Broken

The LORD is near to the brokenhearted
and saves the crushed in spirit.

PSALM 34:18 ESV

They're all around you: the mother whose child just passed away; the grandmother who sits alone in her home, forgotten by family members; the middle school student tormented by her so-called friends; the man sleeping under the bridge; the little boy who is being sexually abused by an uncle.

The world is filled with broken people yearning for wholeness. Along the way, they need people like you—people who are made for a passionate response to the broken. The reason your heart quickens when you see that young mom with no groceries for her kids is because God put His heart inside of you. The reason it hurts so much when you find out a local child has been abused is because God's heart—beating inside of you—is broken. You were born for this, sweet woman of faith. Caring for others is as vital to you as breathing, and it warms the heart of God.

I want to do what I can to help others who are broken, Lord.
Lead me, day by day, to the ones who need me most. Amen.

More Joy in Place of Sorrow

"So also you have sorrow now, but I will see you again, and your hearts will rejoice, and no one will take your joy from you."
JOHN 16:22 ESV

It doesn't make sense. You've been through a tragedy. You should be reeling. Most people would be. But you have this inexplicable sense of peace coursing through your body. Yes, you're sad. Yes, your world has been rocked. But somehow, in the very midst of the pain, you've managed to find joy—the kind you could never have discovered on your own.

God created you to experience true joy—on good days and bad. Perhaps that's one reason laughter and tears are so closely connected. They hover near one another, each ready to activate as needed. And boy, does life ever give you opportunities to need them!

Don't ever be ashamed of your joy—even if it erupts in the middle of a rough season. It's a gift, after all—one you were born to enjoy.

Lord, I'm grateful for the joy that fills my heart. Sometimes it makes no sense. When my world is spinning out of control, I should be weeping. But many times You've stepped in and have given me joy in place of mourning. Thank You! Amen.

More Time in God's Word

So then faith cometh by hearing,
and hearing by the word of God.
ROMANS 10:17 KJV

Cindy loved to read. She devoured book after book—everything from novels to nonfiction self-help books. You could most often find her curled up on the sofa or in her bed with a book in hand. When it came to reading her Bible, though, Cindy wasn't as enthused. She read verses here and there but didn't soak up the Word in the same way she spent time in the books she loved.

Why is that? Perhaps she didn't see her Bible as a giant story-book-like novel. Or maybe the "self-help" features in scripture weren't as easy to understand as a modern text.

The truth is this: you were made to spend time in God's Word. God created you with a need, a desire, to know Him more, and part of the "knowing" comes by getting out your Bible and reading—not just a verse here or there—but whole chapters at a time, in context.

What are you waiting for, sister? Grab that Bible and dive in!

Lord, I'm so grateful for Your Word. The Bible truly is
a lamp to my feet and a light to my path. Thank You
for sharing Your Word with mankind. Amen.

More Strength to the Powerless

He gives power to the weak and
strength to the powerless.
ISAIAH 40:29 NLT

You feel like a limp dishrag. If someone would just wring you out and hang you up to dry, that would be fine with you. You're done—with this day, with the people surrounding you, with your workload, with the laundry—with *everything*. Exhaustion has taken root to the point where everything coming out of your mouth is nonsensical, and all you want to do is take a hot bath and climb into bed.

We all have days when the exhaustion gets to us. Stress. Kids. Messy house. Tough job. Emotional woes. Physical challenges. They threaten to rob us of our last bit of strength. But here's great news: God gives strength to the powerless. Not just any kind of strength, mind you, but supernatural strength. He gives power to the weak.

Picture the teensy-tiniest ant, suddenly muscular and strong enough to defend the whole colony. That's you, even when you don't feel like it. One drop of the Creator's strength and you're ready to tackle giants—even on those days when you'd rather curl up with a good book.

Thank You for Your supernatural
strength, Lord. I really need it! Amen.

More Trust, Less Anxiety

Cast all your anxiety on him because he cares for you.
1 PETER 5:7 NIV

"Lissa, can I ask you a question?"

"Sure." Lissa looked up from her work and into her coworker's eyes. "What's up?"

"I'm just a little worried about you," Frances explained. "You've been working round the clock, and you're always so. . .stressed out. Anxious."

"I'm on deadline, girl. You know that. It's important to the company and important to me. There's nothing wrong with that."

"Maybe, but you have dark circles under your eyes and you've worn that same sweater every day for two weeks."

"It's cold out." Lissa pulled the worn sweater closer. "What does it matter what I look like anyway?"

Okay, so she used to care a lot more about her appearance. And yes, she had been working round the clock. But was it anyone's business, really?

Maybe you can relate. You go, go, go and then wonder why you're completely zapped. You were made for more than work anxieties. God wants you to lay those down and rest in Him. No stress. No angst. Just complete and total relaxation.

There. Doesn't that feel good?

> *Ah, I needed that, Lord! May I learn to lay down*
> *my daily stresses and find rest in You. Amen.*

More Doing of the Word

*Do not merely listen to the word, and so
deceive yourselves. Do what it says.*

JAMES 1:22 NIV

She sat in church every Sunday, heard every message, could even quote the lines of the songs they'd sung. But as soon as seventeen-year-old Traci was outside the walls of the church, none of it really mattered to her. She lived like she wanted, dated who she wanted, ran around with the friends she wanted. In other words, she heard the Word but didn't do it.

God wants you to be a doer, not just a hearer. It's not enough to show up for church, women's Bible study, and the annual women's retreat. It means nothing to memorize verses for the Bible quiz, invite the pastor over for lunch, or bake casseroles for the Wednesday evening meal if the words of the messages aren't penetrating your heart. Yes, those are all good things, but a doer of the Word really takes to heart what she has heard. She changes her attitude, her thinking, the way she treats others. She accepts Jesus—way down deep in her heart.

Are you a hearer or a doer? Only you can answer that question. But either way, you were created to be a doer.

*Lord, I want to follow through. I want to be more than
a hearer, but I'm going to need Your help. Amen.*

More Loving

Some would argue that love is a feeling. You know it when the one you love walks in the room. Your heart swells; your tummy gets butterflies; you can hardly string two sentences together.

But is that really all there is to love?

Love is a verb—an action. And loving people isn't always easy. When that younger brother of yours is addicted to drugs, it's tough. When you live in a home with an angry, aggressive mother, that's difficult. When you've been taken advantage of by someone at work, the last thing you want to do is to love that person.

But God commands us to love. In fact, He designed us to love. And He *expects* us to love, even when it feels impossible. Love doesn't mean you put your stamp of approval on negative behavior. It doesn't mean you extend mushy-gushy words to the one who is off course. It simply means that you exhibit the kind of love God would give you when you've fallen off the straight and narrow. You keep hoping, keep believing, keep trusting.

You were created to love, girl. Get to it!

Help me be more loving, Father, I pray. Amen.

More Prayer

Rejoice always, pray continually, give thanks in all circumstances;
for this is God's will for you in Christ Jesus.
1 THESSALONIANS 5:16–18 NIV

When you begin to fall in love with someone, you can't wait to talk to him. The first few weeks of your relationship are spent in countless hours on the phone or out to dinner, sharing stories, ideas, plans, and dreams. This getting-to-know-you phase is critical and sets the foundation for the romance to come.

As your relationship deepens, so do your conversations. You share from the heart—concerns, joys, even really hard things.

God wants you to spend the kind of time with Him that you would devote to a new love interest. He wants you to be just as excited, just as comfortable, sharing the things you care about and the things that worry you. He will hang on your every word and won't ever let you down.

Prayer time is share time. You share your heart, and God shares His. It's a mutual conversation that will draw you closer together.

Lord, I love our chats. It's so great to get things off my
chest and to get to know You on a deeper level.
Thanks for listening and responding! Amen.

More of the New

*Therefore, if anyone is in Christ, the new creation
has come: The old has gone, the new is here!*

2 CORINTHIANS 5:17 NIV

Maggie turned her home into a shrine of sorts. She had her grandmother's china, her aunt's salt and pepper shaker collection, her father's tools, and her mother's pie plates. Everywhere you looked, there were glimpses of the past—of her loved ones who had gone on to be with the Lord. Before long the clutter from their lives was filling up the place. It started to grate on her husband's nerves. It seemed as though every time he turned around, he tripped over someone else's belongings.

It's one thing to collect physical items from the past and yet another thing altogether to hang tightly to the emotional clutter of days gone by.

When it comes to your spiritual walk, God wants you to release the clutter. Let it go. It's not as easy as holding a garage sale or taking your woes to the secondhand store. This is going to require concerted effort. But getting rid of the pain of the past opens you up to wonderful new things ahead. And doesn't that sound lovely, sister?

*Lord, I want to step out of the past so I'm free to walk
into the future. No clutter holding me back! Amen.*

More Lifting Up Each Other

Two are better than one, because they have a good return for their labor: If either of them falls down, one can help the other up. But pity anyone who falls and has no one to help them up.

ECCLESIASTES 4:9-10 NIV

"You can do it. Don't give up!"

Imagine a runner headed toward the finish line. He's nearly ready to give up. His calves are killing him. His breaths are shallow, erratic. He's so exhausted he can barely think straight. Then, along the side of the road, a group of friends call out to him, "You've got this! Don't stop!" Those words are just enough to propel him forward toward the finish line.

We were made to holler, "Don't give up!" to those who are struggling around us. We are meant to be encouragers. When friends, family members, or coworkers fall, we need to pick them up, dust them off, and say things like, "It's okay! You've got this!"

It's time for believers to look for more opportunities to encourage their loved ones. It's not always easy—especially if the one who has taken the tumble has fallen before in the same way or same area. But do your best to encourage anyway. You were created to be a lifter of heads, hearts, and hands, after all.

Lord, I want to be an encourager to those I love. Show me how, when, and where to lift my voice and urge them on. Amen.

More Peace, Less Anger

Do not be quickly provoked in your spirit,
for anger resides in the lap of fools.
ECCLESIASTES 7:9 NIV

Olivia had every right to be angry. After what her boss did to her—and in front of her coworkers, no less? She should've let him have it. He certainly deserved a tongue-lashing, and she'd been holding it in for months. Nothing would've pleased her more in the moment than cutting loose. Whew! That would've felt great!

But the Lord wouldn't let her lash out. Instead, she spent some time in the ladies' room trying to calm herself down. She paced and poured out her heart to God. It took some time, but He eventually brought peace to her heart and she was able to go on with her day. She would talk to her boss—soon—but not in a heated state. Things would go more smoothly if she collected herself first and addressed him in a peaceful state of mind.

Have you been there? How did you handle the situation? Calming down in the moment is tougher than it looks, but you can do it, sister!

Lord, I was made for more peace (in the moment)
and less emotional outbursts. I know this, but I'll
definitely need Your help with this one! Amen.

More Self-Control

*But the Holy Spirit produces this kind of fruit in our lives: love,
joy, peace, patience, kindness, goodness, faithfulness, gentleness,
and self-control. There is no law against these things!*

GALATIANS 5:22–23 NLT

You know you want it. You know you need it. *Self-control.* It's that
thing that keeps you from eating cookie number three or pie slice
number two. It's the extra *oomph* you need to prevent you from saying that thing that's burning on the tip of your tongue. It's the little
voice in your head that says, "Nope. Don't go there!"

You were made to exercise self-control. That's why it's listed as
one of the fruits of the Spirit. You can't do it on your own—no way.
You need the Spirit of God to hold you back when you feel like
going off on someone who has hurt your kid. You rely on Him to get
you through when you're trying to curb your spending habits. Self-
control is not your enemy; it's your friend, and you were created to
hold hands at every turn.

*Lord, I know You designed me to exhibit more self-control, but
I'm going to need Your help. This doesn't come naturally to me,
I'm afraid. Thanks for stepping in to guide me, Father. Amen.*

More Hope for the Future

"For I know the plans I have for you," says the LORD.
"They are plans for good and not for disaster,
to give you a future and a hope."

JEREMIAH 29:11 NLT

Angela had a hard time seeing the future as anything but a challenge. A single mother of four, she barely made ends meet. For years she'd struggled with the same issues—making rent each month, keeping the lights turned on, and making sure her kids had the food and clothes they needed. Her ex wasn't much help. He was out of work much of the time and provided little, if any, child support.

Maybe you've been in a situation like Angela's that felt hopeless. Any notions about the future seemed idealistic at best. Here's the truth: God created you with more hope for the future. He wants you to get excited about the days ahead, no matter what you're facing today. Tomorrow can—and will—be bright if you keep your focus on Him.

Don't give up. Keep hope alive and look to the future as a brighter place. With the Lord's hand in yours, it surely will be.

Lord, renew my hope for the future! I know You
designed me to be rooted and grounded in hope,
faith, and trust in You. Help me, I pray. Amen.

More Comfort for the Hurting

*"I will comfort you there in Jerusalem
as a mother comforts her child."*

ISAIAH 66:13 NLT

Talia came by it honestly—the feelings of compassion in her heart toward others who were hurting. The elderly woman down the street who lived alone. The little girl whose parents rarely seemed to take the time for her. The coworker who lived in fear. Talia did her best to comfort and console any brokenhearted person who crossed her path. She even went out of her way to bless them with special cards and gifts in the hopes that their spirits would be lifted.

Maybe you're the same; you are filled with compassion for those who need comforting. They touch your heart in ways you simply can't explain. You go out of your way to draw near to those who need love and compassion. You shower them with unexpected blessings. It feels so good!

That desire to comfort comes straight from the heart of your heavenly Father. He placed it inside of you so that others could sense His love and compassion through you.

*Thank You for Your comfort and compassion,
Father! May I receive them and pass them
on to someone in need today. Amen.*

More in the Battle

You have armed me with strength for the battle;
you have subdued my enemies under my feet.
PSALM 18:39 NLT

Battles rage on even when you will them to stop. The war doesn't come to an end simply because you're tired or beaten down from the fighting. But God wants you to know that you are more in the battle. When you're facing enemies (whether invisible or visible), He will give you everything you need to overcome.

Where there is fear, God will give courage. Faith will rise up. Stamina will be there, along with a sincere passion for those who are battling alongside you. And best of all, God has already provided the equipment you need—His armor. Read Ephesians 6 to learn more about the full armor of God; it will keep you safe in the battle.

Here's the key: Don't give up. Don't say, "I just can't." Because you can. With the Lord's hand in yours, you *can*. And you *will*.

Lord, You built me for battle. I'm a she-warrior, moving along
with Your strength, not my own. (Have I admitted how glad
I am it's not my own strength that's required?) Thank You
for the armor and the power to keep going, Father. Amen.

More Mountains Moved

*"You don't have enough faith," Jesus told them. "I tell you
the truth, if you had faith even as small as a mustard seed,
you could say to this mountain, 'Move from here to there,'
and it would move. Nothing would be impossible."*

<small>MATTHEW 17:20 NLT</small>

Obstacles. Marnie saw nothing but obstacles in her way. They loomed like mountains with jagged peaks, stretching to the sky in front of her, casting terrifying shadows below. She shivered with fear as she gazed up at them.

Financial mountains—more bills than paydays.

Relational mountains—more friend drama than she could bear.

Mountains of loss—after the unexpected death of her sister.

Mountains of pain—while battling through a rough flare with autoimmune disease.

Perhaps you've faced mountains like Marnie's. You've stared at them in defeat, convinced you'll never get past them.

God created you to be more than a shadow dweller when mountains rise in your path. You can speak to those mountains and watch them disappear into the sea!

Summon your faith, girl! Open your mouth and speak!

*Lord, today I speak to the mountains in my life. You created
me for this, and I trust Your plan. Mountains, be gone
in the mighty name of Jesus! Amen.*

More Effective Prayers

The LORD is far from the wicked, but he
hears the prayer of the righteous.
PROVERBS 15:29 ESV

Sarah didn't feel as though her prayers were accomplishing much. She poured out her heart to God, but she secretly wondered if He even heard her cries. Were her prayers bouncing off the ceiling, or was the Lord really, truly listening and caring about what she went through? Sarah honestly couldn't tell for sure. But then, she couldn't base such things on feelings, could she? Feelings are fickle, after all.

Maybe you've felt this way at times. You've cried out to the Lord, but answers didn't seem to come—at least not soon enough to make a difference in your situation. It's easy to get discouraged and to stop praying, isn't it?

Oh, but God doesn't want you to give up. He wants your prayer life to be active and vibrant. The more passionate you are in your approach to prayer, the more invested you become. Pray for your needs, of course; but don't forget to spend adequate time praising Him. (God doesn't hear them enough—the praises of His people should ring out daily!)

God hears Your prayers. Don't ever forget that, even when fickle feelings kick in!

Lord, I'm so glad You hear and respond to my prayers.
How grateful I am for our times together, Father. Amen.

More Abiding

*"I am the vine; you are the branches. Whoever abides
in me and I in him, he it is that bears much fruit,
for apart from me you can do nothing."*
JOHN 15:5 ESV

Picture a fisherman sitting on the edge of a river. He baits his hook, then tosses the line out into the water. Then he waits. And waits. Though the midmorning sun beats down on his back, he is not deterred. The fisherman is sure a fish will come along and nibble at his line, but until that happens, he's content to sit and wait, no matter the weather.

God wants you to be like that fisherman. When you dangle your feet over the edge of that proverbial river, He wants you to relax. Bait your hook, toss out your line, then wait on His response. Storms might come. Winds might howl. But you can remain there, safely tucked away, never moving. And all because of God's promise of protection and love.

Abide in Christ. Hang out with Him. Love on Him. You were born to abide.

*Lord, I'm not moving. I'm hanging out with You,
no matter what storms might come. I'll abide, Lord.
Because apart from You, I can do nothing. Amen.*

More Clarity of Vision

Trust in the LORD with all your heart; do not depend on your own understanding. Seek his will in all you do, and he will show you which path to take.

PROVERBS 3:5–6 NLT

Natalie refused to get glasses, even though she knew she needed them. Was it a vanity issue? Maybe. But truthfully, driving was becoming hazardous. And seeing the clock from the far side of the room? Impossible. She could barely make out the billboards on the side of the road either.

When she attended her daughter's choir concert and couldn't distinguish one child from the other, Natalie knew she couldn't put it off any longer. She went to the eye doctor and ordered those much-needed glasses. Immediately the world came into beautiful focus. She could hardly believe all the things she'd been missing—the details on the tree leaves, the razor-sharp images on the TV screen. Wow! What a difference!

God wants you to have more clarity of vision—not just with your physical eyes but with your spiritual ones. He's up to something—can you see it? If not, maybe it's time to peer through your spiritual glasses for a closer look.

You've designed me to see things the way You do, Lord. I'll put on my spiritual glasses and have clear vision from here on out! Amen.

More Blessings

The trustworthy person will get a rich reward, but a
person who wants quick riches will get into trouble.
PROVERBS 28:20 NLT

Marigold got caught in a rainstorm just as she stepped out of the department store. Her car was halfway across the parking lot, and she didn't have an umbrella with her. Oh well. She'd just have to let the showers soak her and dry off when she got home.

Sure enough, the rain had soaked her to the bone by the time she climbed into her car. Marigold glanced in the rearview mirror and laughed. "I look like a drowned rat."

Sometimes the rains come down and drench us like that; at other times, blessings fall at the same rate. We don't even see these gifts coming—and we often feel as if we don't deserve them—but they come, regardless. They shower us all the while we're wondering how we happen to be on the receiving end of so many good things.

God designed you to receive blessings, sister. He has poured out many already, but there are surprises yet to come. Are you ready to receive them?

Lord, I'm so grateful for Your many blessings. My health.
My family. Your provision. I can count on You to shower
many wonderful things down on me, Father. Amen.

More Confession

*If we confess our sins, he is faithful and just to forgive us
our sins and to cleanse us from all unrighteousness.*

1 JOHN 1:9 ESV

"I really don't want to talk about it." Debbie kicked the dirt with the toe of her shoe and stared at the ground.

"Why not?" her best friend asked.

"It's just too. . .hard." To talk about it would mean she had to come clean—and admit her fault. Why would she do that when she could hold it inside? Who was she hurting anyway—besides herself? One day she would admit the truth, and when she did, God would fix things. At least she hoped He would.

Maybe you've been there. You're hanging on to a hidden sin, one you've kept buried beneath the surface. You know it will eventually come out, but for now it's just too hard.

God created you for more than this! You're designed in the image of your forgiving heavenly Father to confess your sins and receive forgiveness. But it can only happen if you're honest about what you've done.

Are you hiding something? It's time to open up and share—truly *share*—what's been covered in cobwebs.

Lord, I don't like peeling back the cobwebs to peer at what's underneath. The things I've done make me shudder. But You've forgiven me, and I'm grateful to have a second chance! Amen.

More Strength for Those Who Hope in God

Be strong and courageous,
*all you who put your hope in the L*ORD*!*
PSALM 31:24 NLT

On a scale of one to ten, Sandy felt like her strength was somewhere in the "two" range. More often than not, she felt zapped—as if every task that needed to be done was just too much. Doing the dishes? Too exhausting. Getting the floors swept? Impossible.

Maybe Sandy's situation sounds extreme to you, but there really are people who struggle to the point of barely being able to get out of bed in the morning. Tasks seem physically overwhelming, so you simply don't do them.

God created you to have strength. Sure, there will be days when the physical interferes—when you have a cold or stomach virus or other bug—but even then He can provide supernatural strength so your body can heal. Even if you're a "Sandy" (someone who genuinely struggles on a daily basis), don't stop asking for God's healing and strength. What you cannot do on your own, He can surely do for you.

Lord, I need Your strength. There are days when I feel I can't
manage, but then You sweep in and supernaturally fill me.
Thank You for creating me to be strong in You! Amen.

More Glimpses of Eternity

Yet God has made everything beautiful for its own time.
He has planted eternity in the human heart, but even so, people
cannot see the whole scope of God's work from beginning to end.
ECCLESIASTES 3:11 NLT

When you're a child, the idea of losing a loved one seems horrifying. You can't imagine doing without your mama or your sister or your grandpa. When you reach your teen years, you hear stories of people passing away—grandparents or even distant relatives—and your life is touched by death. Even then you don't fully understand what heaven is all about or why people actually long for it.

Perhaps glimpses of heaven aren't as real until you fully give your heart to the Lord and have lived long enough to watch loved ones transition into heaven's grasp with smiles on their faces. Until you've watched that elderly mama breathe her last, as she says, "Don't worry! I'll see you again soon!" Talk about perspective!

God wants all of us to experience the joy of heaven. For those who have come to know His Son, Jesus, as Savior, the final destination is guaranteed.

What about you? Have you accepted Jesus as Lord and Savior of your life? Are you headed to the ultimate happily-ever-after? It's not too late—make that decision today!

Lord, I'm so grateful that heaven is mine for the taking
now that I know You as King of my heart! Amen.

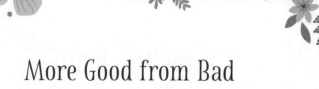

More Good from Bad

We know that God makes all things work together
for the good of those who love Him and are
chosen to be a part of His plan.

ROMANS 8:28 NLV

"Don't worry! God will use it for His glory! What the enemy meant for evil, God will use for good."

If you were raised in church, you probably heard those words a lot. When you lost a job. When your friends deserted you. When illness hit with a vengeance. There you were, in the middle of your struggle, and some well-meaning person had the audacity to say, "Look on the bright side!"

When you're in the middle of a dark season, it's hard to look on the bright side. And sometimes cheerful words from a friend or loved one can feel more like a slap in the face. Don't they get it? You're hurting.

If you're ready to search the Word for yourself, you'll find many references to back up what your loved ones are trying to say. Their delivery might not be the best, but the truth remains: God longs to bring good from the bad in your life. You were created for more victory stories. So instead of getting irritated, take a deep breath and turn to the Word for the encouragement you need.

You designed me to find the good in the bad,
Lord, and I'm doing my best! Amen.

More Possibilities

*Jesus looked at them and said, "This cannot be done
by men. But with God all things can be done."*
MATTHEW 19:26 NLV

"All things."

Ponder those words.

The Bible says that with God, *all things* are possible. (Not just a *few*, but all!) Sicknesses can be healed; lives can be restored; marriages can be mended. Children can obey their parents; students who struggle can make it; friendships that have been severed can be repaired. The possibilities are endless when you trust the Lord with your life circumstances.

If you really viewed your life, your circumstances, and your relationships through the lens of endless possibilities, what would that look like? Would your faith increase? Would your courage deepen? Would your ability to see beyond today grow stronger?

You were made for more possibilities. Don't let the pain of whatever you're trudging through stop you from seeing the possibility of beautiful outcomes. God *can* and *will* redeem. He's working, even now, in your situation. And don't be surprised when a beautiful outcome is revealed!

*Lord, I'm so grateful for possibilities! They give me such
hope for tomorrow. Thank You for being in control of
my life. With You all things are possible! Amen.*

More Confident

*Let us then with confidence draw near to the throne of grace,
that we may receive mercy and find grace to help in time of need.*
HEBREWS 4:16 ESV

Geneva struggled with a lack of confidence. It all started in childhood. She didn't get a lot of encouragement from her parents or teachers, especially in the academic areas where she felt particularly weak and vulnerable. Her confidence also waned in her teens as her grades teetered between Bs and Cs.

When she reached adulthood, she found herself in a constant state of comparison. Was she as pretty as other women? Was she as popular? Would she ever measure up, or would she always be found lacking?

God never intended for his girls to play the comparison game. He wants your confidence to be rooted not in your own abilities or looks but in Him alone.

When and where does your confidence wane? Ask God to show you how to overcome your lack of confidence when it strikes and then turn your gaze to Him. He's the confidence builder, the One you can trust for a heavenly boost. You were created for more of His confidence, sister!

*Lord, I trust in Your confidence, not my own. I draw near
today because I know You'll help me. What I cannot do
alone, You can do through me. I'm so grateful! Amen.*

More Worthy

*To this end we always pray for you, that our God may make
you worthy of his calling and may fulfill every resolve
for good and every work of faith by his power.*

2 THESSALONIANS 1:11 ESV

"You are worthy in His sight."

What do you think of when you read those words? Do you feel worthy? Are you really, truly worthy when you stand before a holy and perfect God?

God created You in His image, and He's a holy, perfect God. You strive for perfection, but it seems elusive at best. But you have to stop viewing yourself through the veil of humanly perfection. You are made righteous—*worthy*—because of the blood of Jesus. When His blood was shed, He covered every indiscretion and every bit of shame you might ever experience. Applying that blood to your life makes you worthy. Yes, it's true! You're worthy because of Him.

Stop struggling with the "Am I good enough for God?" question. You're not. (No human being is!) But through the blood of Jesus Christ, you are.

*I get it, Lord! I'm really not worthy. In and of myself,
I'm flawed and imperfect. But through Your blood, Jesus,
all sins are washed away, and I'm found worthy by You. Amen.*

More Overflow

*Our hope comes from God. May He fill you with joy
and peace because of your trust in Him. May your
hope grow stronger by the power of the Holy Spirit.*
ROMANS 15:13 NLV

Lisa set the mop bucket in the sink and turned on the water to fill it. She turned away for a couple of minutes to take care of one of the kids, and when she turned back, the bucket had overflowed and was filling the sink. If she didn't shut off the water right away, the whole kitchen could flood!

Maybe you've done something like that. You let the bathwater run too long and created a catastrophe, or maybe you turned the sprinkler on in the yard and completely forgot about it for an entire day.

God wants to fill you up—as full as that bucket or bathtub. He wants you to overflow, to spill out onto others. Spill out what, exactly? Love. Joy. Peace. Long-suffering. Goodness. Patience.

Are you spilling over? You were designed for it, sister. Overflow onto those you come in contact with, that they might be drawn to the Lord as well.

Let it flow!

*Lord, thank You for the reminder that Your joy and
peace and blessings overflow in my life. I want to spill
out onto others today, Father! Help me, I pray. Amen.*

More Time Seeking

"You will seek me and find me,
when you seek me with all your heart."

JEREMIAH 29:13 ESV

Remember the parable in the Bible about the woman who lost her coin? She had others, sure. Nine more, in fact. But when she lost one single coin, she went on a search that included lighting a lamp, sweeping the house, and carefully searching until she found what she was looking for.

The diligence of the woman searching for her coin is to be applauded. She didn't give up. We need to be just as diligent when we're searching for the things of God. If we don't understand what we're reading in the Bible, we need to press in and ask the Lord to give us eyes to see. When we're not getting our prayers answered immediately, we must keep praying, keep believing.

You were created to seek and seek and seek some more. You were never designed to be a quitter, no matter how great the temptation. Be diligent, sister! You'll be rewarded in the end.

Lord, I won't give up. I'll keep seeking until
I get the answers I need. Thank You for
reminding me to be persistent. Amen.

More Like God (in Thinking)

"My thoughts are not your thoughts, neither are your ways my ways, declares the LORD."

ISAIAH 55:8 ESV

Deena stared at the portrait of her mother that hung in the front hall of their house.

"You look like her, you know," her father said as he sidled up next to her. "You always have. But now that you're grown up, I see the resemblance even more."

Deena saw it too. She and her mother were dead ringers, to be sure.

The same thing is true of your relationship with God. He wants your thoughts to be so closely aligned with His that people can't tell you apart. All of those heavy, weighted concerns can be lifted as you take on His thoughts.

So what areas do you need to work on? Where do you struggle in your thought life? Do you worry? Fret? Are you overly anxious? Do you replay scenes in your head?

God can help you with all of those things, but you have to give them to Him. He'll scrub those icky thoughts away and give you the mind of Christ—if you ask.

Lord, You said in Your Word that You would give me the mind of Christ. Today I'm asking for that, Lord. No longer will I dwell on my fretful thoughts. From now on, I'll think like You, Lord. Amen.

More Like God (in Actions)

A man of many companions may come to ruin,
but there is a friend who sticks closer than a brother.
PROVERBS 18:24 ESV

"Monkey see, monkey do."

You've probably heard that expression at some point in your life. No matter which "monkeys" you hang out with, you're liable to start acting like them.

Little children excel at it. They learn to walk, talk, and play by mimicking others. And it doesn't stop there! This copycat behavior is especially evident during the teen years when kids glean attitudes and habits from one another.

But it's also true for adults. If you hang out with women who gossip, you'll probably start gossiping. If you hang out with women intent on growing their relationship with the Lord, you'll probably end up stronger in Him.

It's time for a monkey check. Look around your cage and see who is close by. Are they pulling you away from God or pushing you toward Him? You might want to distance yourself from the monkeys who are setting a bad example, if only for a season.

I want to be more like You in the way I act, Lord. I don't
want to embarrass or humiliate You or give You a bad
name. I'll do my best to pull away from the ones who
might deliberately cause me to stumble. Amen.

More Rested

*"Come to me, all you who are weary and
burdened, and I will give you rest."*
MATTHEW 11:28 NIV

Frazzled. That was the only word Veronica could think of to describe
how she felt most of the time. *Frazzled. Worn out. Exhausted.* Between
her job, the house, the kids, and her volunteer work at church, she
barely had time to sleep, let alone take a day for herself. Before long
her body crashed. She ended up sick and was forced to take a few
days off, whether she wanted to or not.

God created your body to rest. He instituted the Sabbath, knowing the inclination of mankind to keep going, even past the breaking
point. If you really take time off—to recharge, renew, and sleep—you'll
get more accomplished. If you don't take time to rest, you'll eventually
collapse. Things will spiral downward.

Say these words to yourself and mean them: "He created me to
rest more!"

And then get some rest, sister!

*I've been burdened, Lord. I've been weary. But You see,
You understand, and You're here to help me get
the rest I need. Thank You, Father. Amen.*

More Reproof

All Scripture is breathed out by God and profitable for teaching, for reproof, for correction, and for training in righteousness, that the man of God may be complete, equipped for every good work.
2 TIMOTHY 3:16–17 ESV

If you're like most people, you're not a big fan of correction. You'd rather people not tell you how to become a better version of yourself, thank you very much. Why don't they just mind their business and focus on their own flaws?

The truth is, we're all going to face scrutiny in this life. We have to learn to be okay with correction when it's due or we won't know how to handle it when it's not.

So how do you react when corrected by a boss, a friend, or a coworker? Do you handle it graciously or knee-jerk? Do you pick the meat and toss the bones or toss the whole thing because you're offended?

Believe it or not, God created you for more reproof. He is shaping you into the woman you will become, and that can happen only if you admit to your flaws and continue to grow.

More reproof. It's part of God's plan. So, deep breath, girl. Yes, criticism is headed your way, but you can bear it—and grow from it.

*Lord, I'll do my best to handle critiques
when they come my way. Amen.*

More Pressing

Not that I have already obtained this or am
already perfect, but I press on to make it my own,
because Christ Jesus has made me his own.
PHILIPPIANS 3:12 ESV

We strive for perfection but will never reach it in this lifetime. We do our best to look attractive—adding makeup, fixing our hair, and dressing in nice clothes. We attempt to do our best work in school—to earn good grades and impress the teacher. We even shoot for the stars when it comes to our careers. Nothing but the best for us—or so we hope.

God loves it when we give our best, but He isn't looking for perfection. He just wants us to care about the things (and people) He cares about.

If we press toward anything, may it be toward Him. If we strive to be anything, let it be more like our Savior. If we push to spend more time at something, let it be at developing our prayer and worship life. These are the kinds of "pressings" that honor our heavenly Father.

Lord, I press in close to You today. I deliberately tune
out all distractions and focus solely on You. To be
like You, Lord, is my deepest desire. Amen.

More Walking by Faith

For we walk by faith, not by sight.
2 CORINTHIANS 5:7 ESV

Poor Hansel and Gretel. They dropped crumbs all along the path, hoping to find their way back home again. Unfortunately, the crumbs were eaten by birds, and they were lost in the woods indefinitely.

When you lose your way—when the "crumbs" aren't evident—how do you respond? Do you panic? Do you sit beneath a shade tree and give up?

God wants you to trust Him, even when you're feeling lost, even when there's not a scrap of bread to guide you to the right path. He wants you to look to Him—and Him alone—so that He can guide you exactly where you need to go. No fear. No questions. Just faith in the One who knows your path better than you ever could.

God designed you to walk by faith, girl. What's stopping you?

Lord, I will walk by faith. More and more, I'll let go of the reins of my life, Father, and trust You with the details—even when I'm not sure where You're taking me. I trust You, Lord. Amen.

More Successful Plans

May he give you the desire of your heart
and make all your plans succeed.

PSALM 20:4 NIV

"God wants me to be a success?" Stephanie scratched her head as she pondered the notion. "How do you know?"

"Because," her friend replied, "He longs to give you the desires of your heart, and the Bible says that He wants to make your plans succeed."

"Really?" Stephanie said. "Well, that changes everything!"

Wow, that's really something, isn't it? You were created to succeed. Think about that for a moment. The God of the universe wants you—yes, little old you!—to accomplish great and mighty things. You're His daughter, after all. Would you, as a parent, want anything less than success for your beloved child?

So, don't give up. Don't succumb to feelings of failure. You're *not* a failure; you were made for success, girl. Now, dress for it—inside and out.

You have plans for my success, Lord. I can't see them yet,
but I know I can trust You. Today I give all my hopes, plans,
and dreams to You. Do with them as You will. Amen.

More Generosity

"But who am I, and who are my people, that we should be able to give as generously as this? Everything comes from you, and we have given you only what comes from your hand."

1 CHRONICLES 29:14 NIV

God created you to be more generous. Don't you love that? If you're a giver, then you already know it's more blessed to give than to receive. But what if you had more so that you could give more? What if you were able to stock an elderly neighbor's pantry or cover the cost of a doctor visit for a friend with no insurance? What if you could sponsor a teen on a mission trip or support a child in a third world country?

The more you give, the more you want to give. The more you bless others, the more you are blessed in return (and not just monetarily). It feels so good to meet others' needs. Your heart will be stirred as never before.

Brace yourself, sister. Open your eyes and your heart! God is going to use you to give in ways you never dreamed possible.

Lord, I want to give all I can to help those in need and to share Your love with others. Show me creative ways that I can be generous with all You've given me, Father. Amen.

More of God's Patience toward You

The Lord is not slow to fulfill his promise as some count
slowness, but is patient toward you, not wishing that any
should perish, but that all should reach repentance.

2 PETER 3:9 ESV

Patience. . .patience! Having patience is hardly ever easy.

But wait. Isn't that what God grants you (usually when you don't deserve it)? If He's generous enough to pour out patience on your behalf, then extending it to others is the least you can do! God designed you to be more patient, you know. Don't believe it? Check out the many references to patience in the scriptures.

Don't give up just because something isn't happening according to your timetable. Don't say things like, "I guess God just didn't hear my prayer," or "I guess the Almighty doesn't care about the things that matter to me."

He does care. In fact, He cares enough to build a little character in you while you wait. Hang tight. You were made for more patience, sister. Start showing it!

Lord, I'll try to hold on a little longer. I can't
do it in my strength, but You can give me all I
need to hold tight through the waiting. Amen.

More Time Gazing at Him

One thing I have asked from the Lord, that I will look for: that I may live in the house of the Lord all the days of my life, to look upon the beauty of the Lord, and to worship in His holy house.

PSALM 27:4 NLV

Tina was crushing on a boy in her language arts class. She had a hard time focusing on the teacher because her gaze kept lingering on the handsome guy to her right. He didn't seem to notice she existed. Or did he? Once or twice he looked her way—possibly trying to figure out why she kept staring at him. But she would quickly glance away, her cheeks hot with embarrassment.

Odds are, when you were a high school student, you experienced something similar. You couldn't stop drooling over Mr. Right for Me. You would have done nearly anything to catch his eye, but the whole thing seemed pointless—and he seemed clueless.

Here's some good news! God is not clueless. And right now—at this very moment, in fact—His gaze is solidly locked on yours. He longs to woo you, to spend time with you, to give you all His love. He won't look away or roll His eyes if your gaze stays on Him a minute too long. He adores you! You were made for more time gazing at Him.

I was made to adore You, Lord! So I'll keep gazing at You. You're my everything! Amen.

More Good Deeds

And let us consider how we may spur one another on toward love and good deeds, not giving up meeting together, as some are in the habit of doing, but encouraging one another—and all the more as you see the Day approaching.

HEBREWS 10:24-25 NIV

Remember the line in *The Wizard of Oz* where the Tin Man is told he is a "good deed doer"? Perhaps you've known a few of those in your life. They care for the needy; they pass out clothing and food to the homeless; they provide scholarships for kids to go to college; they tend to the needs of the sick and the elderly. In short, they're amazing, giving people who are "others" focused.

Did you know that God wants you to be a good deed doer too? You were created to perform more—and more!—good deeds. And the longer you walk with Christ, the more natural these actions will become.

We're meant to "spur one another on" toward love and good deeds. Are you encouraging others to be a giver by giving yourself? Are you showing them how to care for the downtrodden by caring yourself?

There's so much more in you, sister. Give—and then give some more.

*Show me fun, creative ways to spread joy
to others with good deeds, Lord! Amen.*

More Heart Strength

My flesh and my heart may fail, but God is the
strength of my heart and my portion forever.
PSALM 73:26 NIV

Presley felt like giving up. She'd worked so hard on this presentation for her boss, only to have the computer swallow it whole at the last minute. All those hours of preparation gone in an instant. She wasn't sure if she should cry or throw something at the wall. In that moment, piecing things together again—from scratch—seemed impossible. She just didn't have the wherewithal to pull it off.

Presley pushed the laptop aside and picked up the phone to call her boss. He would be furious, but what could she do? Before dialing his number, Presley released a slow breath. A glance at the clock showed her it was 8:30. If she worked really hard and really fast, she could probably redo the whole project by midnight—in plenty of time for the meeting.

And that's what she did. Her second go-round went smoother than the first; and the following morning, she made a stellar presentation.

Maybe you've been in a similar situation. Something needs your immediate attention and your heart just isn't in it. God can give you the "oomph" to make it through, even when you're completely convinced you can't. Just ask Him!

I need Your "oomph" today, Lord! Thank You! Amen.

More Reflection

*Now that which we see is as if we were looking in a
broken mirror. But then we will see everything. Now I
know only a part. But then I will know everything in a
perfect way. That is how God knows me right now.*

1 CORINTHIANS 13:12 NLV

Pause. Reflect. Don't rush. Give it time.

There. That wasn't so hard, was it?

We get in such a hurry that we rarely take the time to pause and reflect, but more of Jesus means more time in reflection. "Reflecting on what?" you ask. His goodness. His kindness to you when you don't deserve it. His provision. His love. His exquisite tenderness toward you—when you get it right, and even when you get it wrong.

It's also good to reflect on the areas of your life that need change. Adjustment. When you really take the time to see the problem areas, you will be more likely to take the time to change them.

You were made for more reflection, sister. Never be ashamed to slow down and take all the time you need.

*I need time today, Lord—time to pause
from busyness and reflect on You. Amen.*

More Families

"These commandments that I give you today are to be on your hearts. Impress them on your children. Talk about them when you sit at home and when you walk along the road, when you lie down and when you get up."

Deuteronomy 6:6-7 NIV

God designed us to live and work in units. Families, friends, coworkers—all levels of relationship are part of the Lord's plan. If you're keeping to yourself more than you should, it might be time to nudge open the doors of communication with those around you. And remember—you're not just here to enjoy those kids and grand-kids; the Lord has also designed you to be a legacy-leaver. The little ones are watching you closely, ready to learn from your example. You have a lot to share, and they have much to learn.

Pass down the things of God to those who've been given to you. Teach them His ways. Share His Word. And don't forget you're still on a learning curve too. You likely have family members who can pour into you as you pour into others.

Lord, I want to be a mentor, a loving gift giver. Thank You for surrounding me with "family"—whether blood related or not. I'm grateful for those who love me. Amen.

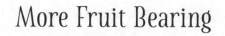

More Fruit Bearing

*"Blessed is the one who trusts in the LORD, whose confidence is
in him. They will be like a tree planted by the water that sends
out its roots by the stream. It does not fear when heat comes;
its leaves are always green. It has no worries in a year
of drought and never fails to bear fruit."*

JEREMIAH 17:7-8 NIV

Elsie moved into a new house with a lemon tree in the backyard. She
could hardly wait for spring so she could pick lemons and use them
for cooking, baking, and making lemonade. Yum!

Unfortunately, the tree didn't produce any fruit that first year.
Or the second. Elsie was disappointed and turned to the internet
for advice. There she learned that lemon trees take their time before
bearing fruit.

And so she began to tend to the tree—to prune it, to make sure
it was fertilized and watered. Her work paid off when lemons burst
to life the third year.

Maybe you're like Elsie. You've planted seeds in a loved one—
prayers, thoughtful deeds, and more—and you don't see fruit yet. In
fact, you're wondering if your proverbial lemon tree is ever going to
produce fruit.

Don't give up! You'll bear fruit in God's perfect season!

*Lord, I won't give up! I want to bear
fruit for Your kingdom. Amen.*

More Opportunities
to Build Up Others

*Therefore encourage one another and build
each other up, just as in fact you are doing.*
1 THESSALONIANS 5:11 NIV

Bella had a hard time bragging on and celebrating the accomplishments of others. She sang her own praises—a lot. But when it came to building up that friend who'd just received a work promotion or whose son just won the MVP trophy in baseball, she just couldn't seem to formulate the words.

It wasn't that she wasn't happy for them, exactly. But the advancement of others sometimes made her feel like she was something of a loser. And she hated that feeling.

Maybe you can relate. You're happy when good things happen for those you love. Mostly. But sometimes all the accolades they receive make you feel "less than."

God created you to sing the praises of your loved ones—to make a big splash when they've done something awesome. You were designed to encourage more, love more, and build up others in good times and bad. Shifting your eyes off yourself is step one. Step two: start encouraging others!

*Lord, help me take my eyes off myself so that
I can sing the praises of others today. Amen.*

More Plans Established

*Commit to the LORD whatever you do,
and he will establish your plans.*

PROVERBS 16:3 NIV

Fiona and her husband bought an old fixer-upper in an established neighborhood they loved. It needed a lot of work inside and out, but they didn't mind. In fact, they could hardly wait to get started. First, they had to tear out the old to make room for the new. Then the most important part: they hired an architect to draw up plans for the new layout.

Once the plans were finalized, the building could begin. They were thrilled to see their new home blossom into a thing of beauty. Wow! Talk about a transformation!

Maybe you're wondering why some areas of your life haven't blossomed into something beautiful. Perhaps it's because you haven't handed the planning of those areas over to the Lord. He's the best architect of all; you'll never be able to draw up plans that come close to His. He has every nook and cranny designed specifically with you in mind.

*Lord, I commit myself to Your plans. I've tried doing things
my way, and the outcome is never quite what I expect.
Do with me as You will, great Architect! Amen.*

More Honor

[Love] does not dishonor others, it is not self-seeking,
it is not easily angered, it keeps no record of wrongs.
1 CORINTHIANS 13:5 NIV

As a child, Lena had a hard time honoring her parents. For whatever reason, her responses to them were often catty and challenging. She couldn't seem to bring herself to willingly submit to their authority. *Everything* was a fight.

As she got older, Lena had a hard time in other relationships too. She struggled to hold down a job because she found fault in every boss. She battled romantic relationships. As soon as someone got too close—or expected too much of her—she bolted. No way was she going to submit to another human being.

Perhaps you've struggled in this area too. You have a hard time bringing honor to others; putting another person above yourself feels unnatural. God designed you to bring honor to Him, to yourself, and to those around you. Ask, and He will show you how to honor them in a way that pleases His heart and draws them closer to Him—and you.

Lord, I give up! My communication style is so
messed up sometimes. I want to honor others
and You. Please show me how, I pray. Amen.

More Desires of Your Heart

Be happy in the Lord. And He will give
you the desires of your heart.
PSALM 37:4 NLV

If someone were to ask, "What are your deepest, fondest desires in life?" how would you answer? Most of us don't think we'll get the things we hope for, so we're afraid to voice them aloud. Or maybe we're worried we *will* get what we desire and won't be able to handle it!

You were created to receive the things you desire, but it's clear (based on this verse from Psalm 37) that the key is found in delighting in the Lord. When you're in relationship with Him—when you place your love for Him above all else—then your desires fall into alignment with what He wants for your life. In other words, they're safe, healthy, God-breathed desires.

Don't be afraid to ask the Lord for the things that you feel called to have—a family, friends, a good job, and so on. He might just surprise you with the ways He fulfills those desires, so be ready! God has an amazing imagination, after all.

I trust You with my desires, Lord. You know best,
so I ask You to fulfill my hopes, wishes, and dreams
in ways that only You can, Father! Amen.

More Understanding

Whoever is patient has great understanding,
but one who is quick-tempered displays folly.

PROVERBS 14:29 NIV

Maybe you've heard the expression "Try to see it from my point of view." People always say this when they think you're being unreasonable or self-focused, don't they? It's not easy to take your eyes off your personal perspective, but when you shift points of view—when you *really* try to see a situation through the eyes of the other person, you have to admit that things look quite different.

What situations are you experiencing today? Do you need a point-of-view shift? Have you been too self-focused? Is it time to give more consideration to someone else?

God wants you to love and care for others the same way you love and care for yourself. So offer more understanding to those you love. Give them the benefit of a thoughtful response when they speak to you (even if you're not a fan of their tone). God will honor your understanding!

Lord, You've made me to be more understanding.
Obviously I'm going to need help with this one!
Help me in this moment, I pray. Amen.

More Power from the Spirit

*May the God of hope fill you with all joy and peace
as you trust in him, so that you may overflow with
hope by the power of the Holy Spirit.*

ROMANS 15:13 NIV

Kerri felt like a spiritual wimp most of the time. Whenever the enemy would rear his ugly head, she would cower in the corner. No show of strength. No mustering of courage. Just *defeat*—often before the battle even got underway.

God never intended our spiritual journey to be one of defeat. We were made for more power from the Holy Spirit. We've been given authority in the name of Jesus to combat the evils of this world, so we must take action when the enemy attempts to steal, kill, or destroy. We have to take a warrior's stance—no apologies!

Are you feeling the power of the Spirit today? If not, ask for it! The more you ask the Spirit of God to fill you, the stronger you'll be. And sister, you were created to be *very* strong in Him!

*Lord, I'm stronger than I know! Through the
power of Your Spirit, I can do great and
mighty things for You. Amen.*

More Difference Making

Do not let yourselves get tired of doing good.
If we do not give up, we will get what is
coming to us at the right time.
GALATIANS 6:9 NLV

"You've really got to stop feeding the homeless and focus more on yourself," Kendra's best friend said after clucking her tongue. "I can't remember the last time I saw you dressed up with proper makeup. You're too busy caring for others to pay attention to the things that matter anymore."

Ouch. Kendra had a hard time swallowing that well-intentioned statement. Maybe you would have had a hard time too. After all, God created us to do good things for others. Helping your elderly parents. Caring for a little one who is sick. Feeding the homeless or ministering to victims of sex trafficking. These are all things that help the world become a better place.

Sure, it's important to keep things in balance in your life. And maybe you really do need to pull back a little and wait for a better season. Ask God what He would have you do. But even if He tells you to wait, there's plenty of time (and opportunity!) to do good things for others.

If you don't take action, who will?

Lord, I want to make a difference in the world. I know You've created me for this. Show me when to slow down and when to speed up. I want to follow Your leading as I do great things for You. Amen.

More Guidance

*He refreshes my soul. He guides me along
the right paths for his name's sake.*
PSALM 23:3 NIV

Melissa loved her car's built-in GPS. She couldn't imagine doing without it. Then, suddenly, she didn't have a choice. When her company flew her to California for a conference, she rented a car on the cheap. The low-end model didn't come with GPS, and she was in an unfamiliar place—Los Angeles. Lost and alone, she had to rely on her phone. Only one problem: it was difficult to drive and manage the phone at the same time. In the end, she had to pull over into a parking lot, look up the address of her destination, and do her best to get there on her own.

God created us with a destination in mind. He puts us on paths and guides us to where we need to go. We can't always see what's coming (and that's often for our benefit), but we know we can trust Him.

What path are you on right now? Can you sense God's guidance? He's right there, leading you every step of the way. You can trust Him—even when you can't see what's coming.

*Lord, I trust You! You're the best GPS out
there. You give guidance in every area
of my life, and I'm so grateful. Amen.*

More Abundance

*Now to him who is able to do immeasurably more than
all we ask or imagine, according to his power that is at
work within us, to him be glory in the church and in Christ
Jesus throughout all generations, for ever and ever! Amen.*

EPHESIANS 3:20–21 NIV

Most of Trina's siblings and cousins had no trouble coming up with a Christmas wish list. They wrote down dozens of items—everything from the latest, greatest electronic gadgets to their favorite dolls and toys.

Not Trina though. She couldn't seem to make herself "wish" for anything. It seemed almost selfish. So she thought about a wish list until she finally managed to write down one or two meager ideas for things that weren't terribly expensive. Her mom was startled and asked her to rethink the list.

Sometimes we approach God like Trina approached her Christmas list. We're afraid to ask Him for the big stuff, so we shrug and say, "Whatever You think, God. Don't put Yourself out."

Oh, but He wants to put Himself out for you! One of the Lord's greatest desires is to lavish His children with unexpected treasures and joys. So don't be surprised when He goes exceedingly, abundantly above all you could ask or think. That's the kind of God He is!

*I'm so grateful I can come to You with everything, Lord—
as my wishes and dreams are nothing compared to
the plans You have in store for me! I can't wait
to see what You have up Your sleeve! Amen.*

More Promises Fulfilled

"When you pass through the waters, I will be with you;
and when you pass through the rivers, they will not sweep
over you. When you walk through the fire, you will not
be burned; the flames will not set you ablaze."
Isaiah 43:2 NIV

Have you been through rough seasons in your life? Have you trudged through waters so deep you thought you might drown? Have you faced fiery trials so fierce you felt you might be consumed?

Life is filled with challenges, but perhaps these rough seasons are when we're best able to see God's hand at work. In the deep waters, His promise remains: you will not drown. When the flames lap at you, and the heat in your face is more than you can stand, still He whispers, "You will not be burned."

God's promises will be fulfilled in your life, no matter how deep the valleys may seem. When He says it, He means it. You were created to see fulfillment of His promises, so hold on tight! He has big things planned for you, sister!

Lord, sometimes I think I've gotten so used to disappointments
that I stop expecting fulfillment of promises. People have let me
down, but You never will. What wonderful news, Father! Amen.

More Possibilities

"What do you mean, 'If I can'?" Jesus asked.
"Anything is possible if a person believes."
MARK 9:23 NLT

Have you ever listened to someone who laid out a "what if" scenario that seemed plausible? On and on they went, talking about the what-ifs. At the end of their story, you shrugged and said, "I guess that's possible."

Life is filled with possibilities. Many, many wonderful things could happen if only we believed. Lives could be restored. Relationships could be mended. Finances could be fixed. Shattered hearts could be put back together. The possibility of all these things happening rises exponentially as your faith grows.

What possibilities are you facing today? Which ones are you saying, "Yes and amen!" to? Which ones have you given up on entirely? Have you ever secretly wondered if there's any chance at all?

It's time to trust God with the what-ifs. The possibilities are endless when you place the outcome of life's unique situations into His hands. His hands can handle anything!

Lord, I'm opening my mind to the possibility that You can
turn things around in any situation You choose. My eyes
are wide open as I anticipate miracles all around me. Amen.

More of His Doing, Less of Yours

For by grace you have been saved through faith.
And this is not your own doing; it is the gift of God,
not a result of works, so that no one may boast.
EPHESIANS 2:8-9 ESV

"It all depends on me." How many times have you spoken those words (or at least thought them)? Women who carry the weight of the world on their shoulders often feel they need to fix everything—that they're responsible for everything.

What about you? Are you drowning with the weight of responsibility? If so, then welcome this wonderful truth to your weary spirit: God made you for more of His doing and less of your own. It's not up to you; in fact, it never was. The heavenly Father created you to trust Him to fix things that seem unfixable, stitch tears that seem irreparable, and mend broken hearts that seem forever shattered.

None of the "fixing" is your responsibility—any more than salvation is of your doing. If you could fix everything (Wow, picture it!), you'd be so prideful sharing all the amazing things you accomplished.

But you didn't accomplish them—the heavenly Father did! And it's a lot easier to brag on Him than on yourself, for sure!

It's Your doing, Lord. Not mine. Whew! What a relief. Amen.

More Humility

Do nothing out of selfish ambition or vain conceit.
Rather, in humility value others above yourselves.
PHILIPPIANS 2:3 NIV

Billboards, magazine ads, TV commercials, and infomercials all scream the praises of me, myself, and I. We're expected to take utmost care of ourselves—our hair, clothing, skin, and makeup—and on top of that, have the very best of everything. Why? Because we deserve it—*all* of it!

But the reality is it's not all about us. If you read the Bible carefully, you'll notice that the world's message just isn't true. Does that mean it's wrong to take care of your skin, hair, and body? Of course not. God wants you to honor the vessel He has given you. But He's not keen on you spending all day hyper-focused on that stuff. Is it essential to have the newest, fastest cars, the latest technology, or a job you can brag about? Not really. Why? Because you were designed to be humble, to do nothing out of selfish ambition or vain conceit. You were called by God to value others above yourself. It's not always easy—especially when it comes to the "stuff" you want—but it's always right.

Lord, I have nothing to prove—to my neighbors,
my friends, or even myself. I humble myself today
and ask that Your will be done in my life. Amen.

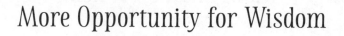

More Opportunity for Wisdom

*Be very careful, then, how you live—not as
unwise but as wise, making the most of every
opportunity, because the days are evil.*
EPHESIANS 5:15-16 NIV

Did you realize that wisdom is a choice you have to make? Several times a day you'll be presented with opportunities to decide: do I choose wisely or foolishly?

God designed you for more wisdom, sister. He doesn't want His reputation to be ruined because you—His representative here on earth—lived in a way that dishonored Him or made Him look bad to others. When you live as one who is wise, you bring honor to God and to yourself.

Be careful how you live. Make the most of every opportunity. Why? Because the world is watching—people are looking to you to lead by example. You say you're a Christian, and they want to see if your actions and words match up.

Are you operating in godly wisdom? That's *exactly* what the world needs to see.

*Lord, I want to honor You by choosing wisdom
in every situation. I know others are watching.
Help me to make the right choices, I pray. Amen.*

More Chains Broken

*About midnight Paul and Silas were praying
and singing hymns to God, and the other
prisoners were listening to them.*

ACTS 16:25 NIV

Carolina was done with smoking. She had decided never to take another puff—after this last cigarette anyway. But the next time temptation hit, she found herself giving in—again. Afterward she felt awful, riddled with guilt and remorse.

Maybe you've battled addictions too. You've felt chained to cigarettes. Or alcohol. Or sugar. You couldn't stop lying, cheating, stealing. . . . The vices are real, and they keep you bound up until you can hardly breathe.

Chains are deadly at times. They hook you and refuse to let go. You're like a dog tethered to a spike in the yard, the chain getting all twisted up as you fight to free yourself.

God longs for you to be set free, dear one—not just from the obvious addictions, but others as well. Bitterness. Hatred. Jealousy. These are all chains that can keep you in bondage.

You weren't created for chains—you were made for more than that. God created you to be set free from all the things that seek to bind you.

*Lord, I'm done! I want to be set free—permanently!
Help me to exercise the self-control You've given
me. Break every chain I pray, Father. Amen.*

More Attitude Checks

For the word of God is alive and active. Sharper than any double-edged sword, it penetrates even to dividing soul and spirit, joints and marrow; it judges the thoughts and attitudes of the heart.

HEBREWS 4:12 NIV

Cindy could be a little on the, well, snippy side. She didn't mean to be, but her curt behavior often caught others off guard. When Cindy was a child, her mother would often say, "Check your attitude, Cindy!" Only one problem: she didn't know how. She would try, but then her temper would flare all over again.

Over the years, God showed Cindy how to keep her temper in check and how to treat others kindly, even when she didn't feel like it. All she had to do was imagine how Jesus would respond. Once she caught a glimpse of it in her mind, the rest was easy.

What about you? Do others in your world have to mutter the words "Attitude check!" whenever you come around? If so, it's time to see people through the eyes of Jesus. No one in the history of, well, *ever*, had to ask Jesus to check His attitude!

Lord, I don't want to be known for needing frequent attitude checks. I want the mind and attitude of Christ. Help me with that, I pray. Amen.

More Opportunities to Forgive

Be kind and compassionate to one another,
forgiving each other, just as in Christ God forgave you.
EPHESIANS 4:32 NIV

"You don't understand!" Sally cried out. "She hurt my feelings. . .*again.* And this time I know it was on purpose. So don't expect me to forgive her. She'll just turn around and do it all over again like she always does."

"You don't know that, honey," her mother said. "Sometimes people hurt others without meaning to."

"I'm never going to forgive her, and you can't make me!" Sally stormed off to her bedroom.

Maybe you can relate to Sally's predicament. Forgiving someone who is a repeat offender is especially difficult. Patterns of mistreatment need to be broken. But know that it is possible to break unhealthy ties to a person and still forgive them. In fact, you *must* forgive them—even someone who has done the unforgivable. To hold a person in unforgiveness is to hold yourself in prison—and that's no way to live, girl.

Lord, You've given me ample opportunities to forgive people
for the pain they've caused me, and today I choose to do
just that. Show me how to forgive even now, Father. Amen.

More Soaring Like Eagles

But those who trust in the LORD will find new strength.
They will soar high on wings like eagles. They will run
and not grow weary. They will walk and not faint.

ISAIAH 40:31 NLT

Have you ever watched a baby bird take flight for the first time? The mama gently nudges it to the edge of the nest, and then—*whoosh!* Off he goes, soaring through the sky, wings flapping, the rest of the birdie babies cheering him on.

In many ways, the faith walk is a bit like that bird taking to flight. You spend more time worrying about hitting the ground than enjoying the view sometimes. But God designed you to soar like an eagle. There should be more cloud surfing than ground hugging.

What areas of your life are shaky right now? Finances? Relationships? Health? You're like that baby bird, even now—just trust that your wings really do work. *They do!* They were given to you by your heavenly Father, and He plans for you to soar like an eagle no matter what you're facing. So don't wait, little bird. Let's fly!

Lord, I won't sit in the nest any longer. I won't let fear
hold me back. I'll trust in You, and I'll soar over
my circumstances! Watch me fly! Amen.

More Gentleness

*But the Holy Spirit produces this kind of fruit in our lives: love,
joy, peace, patience, kindness, goodness, faithfulness, gentleness,
and self-control. There is no law against these things!*

Galatians 5:22–23 nlt

Perhaps you've used the expression "She handled it with kid gloves."
This expression stems from the 1700s, when gloves were made from
kid goat leather. To handle something "with kid gloves" means you
treat it delicately. Very carefully. Gingerly.

Imagine you're been tasked with carrying a single ostrich egg
from one side of a football field to another. You'd handle it with kid
gloves, hands trembling all the way, until you safely delivered it to
its destination.

Now imagine that you have a situation as delicate as that egg. It's
going to require delicacy. Gentleness. Great care. You manage it just
fine—in part because you thought it through in advance. You made a
decision to be gentle at any cost.

God designed you to be gentler—with your family, your boss, your
pets, even yourself. Choose today to handle all of those (and more!)
with greater care than ever before.

*Lord, I'll be gentle! I'll use kid gloves to take care of the people
You've placed in my life. They're more valuable to me than
anything, so I'll treat them with love and kindness. Amen.*

More of His Steadfast Love and Faithfulness

The LORD passed before him and proclaimed, "The LORD, the LORD, a God merciful and gracious, slow to anger, and abounding in steadfast love and faithfulness."

EXODUS 34:6 ESV

Trish was in a tough marriage. About half of the time, her husband, Tim, was loving and kind. The other half? Well, he would become frustrated or accusatory, even cold and withdrawn. She didn't know what to make of it. Did he love her or didn't he? After sixteen years of marriage, she wasn't sure anymore.

Human relationships, even marriages, can be fickle. Opinions about love change as feelings shift. God never intended for us to live this way; He has always longed for His children to love as He loves—and this requires steadfastness and faithfulness.

You'll never need to wonder if God loves you. He did; He does; and He always will. He abounds in love toward you, and that won't shift based on anyone's emotions. Best of all, He designed you to receive this love on days when you're feeling it and on days when you're not.

Hopefully you're feeling it today, because He's right there, arms extended, ready to pour it out on you—ready or not.

I'm ready for more of that steadfast love and faithfulness, Lord. Bring it on! Amen.

More Light for Your Path

Your word is a lamp for my feet, a light on my path.
PSALM 119:105 NIV

Marsha had always been told that eyes automatically adjusted to darkness. Stumbling across the pitch-dark hotel room, she wasn't so sure. And when she caught her toe on the edge of the bedframe, she was less sure than ever. So much for adjusting!

The truth is, we all need light to guide our paths. Stumbling around in the dark is no fun, whether you're in an unfamiliar hotel room or on a proverbial journey down life's highway.

The tiniest bit of light can point out bumps in the road, snakes slithering along your path, or even upturned cobblestones.

God's Word is the light believers need to guide our path toward Him. It illuminates the path ahead of us and give us wisdom, peace, and more guidance than any GPS system. You were designed for more of that heavenly glow. You were created to follow that light and to trust His plan—even in unfamiliar places.

Let Him be your guide. You'll be so glad you took the journey!

*Shine that light bright, Lord! I don't want to miss it.
I'll follow Your lead in all things. Amen.*

More Overflowing

You prepare a table before me in the presence of my enemies;
you anoint my head with oil; my cup overflows.
PSALM 23:5 ESV

"Surprise!"

Donna looked around the room, completely shocked. A surprise birthday party—for her? Off in the distance, she saw her best friend from college. What in the world? And her coworkers? How had they pulled this off without her knowing? She glanced at her children—all four of them—and smiled. They, along with their dad's help, had planned this wonderful surprise. And Donna couldn't have been more grateful. Her heart was overflowing with gratitude and love. And judging from the broad smiles on their faces, they were absolutely delighted too.

Maybe you've felt this way over an unexpected surprise. You've been so overwhelmed (in a good way) that your heart seemed to burst with joy. That overflow spilled onto everyone you came in contact with. Talk about a joy encounter!

God designed you for more of those, sister! When it comes to blessings, He loves to surprise His kids. So keep your eyes open! He's sure to delight you with even more.

Lord, my heart is full to overflowing, thanks to You
and Your many blessings. How can I ever thank
You, Father? My cup overflows! Amen.

More Rivers of Delights

They feast on the abundance of your house, and you
give them drink from the river of your delights.
PSALM 36:8 ESV

If you've seen the Willy Wonka movie, you have some idea of what Oompa Loompa Land looks like. It's a wonderland of edible delights—suckers, wrapped candies, and so much more—with a gooey chocolate river flowing through the center of it. (Sounds amazing, right?)

God's river of delights makes the Oompa Loompa river pale in comparison. One day when you spend eternity in heaven with Him, you'll see it fully. When that day comes, you'll discover what you were destined for all along—more of every good thing. Anything you could have dreamed of will be there times ten thousand! All you have longed for will be found inside the gates of heaven—streets of gold, gates of pearl, and mansions that will make our earthly homes look like cracker boxes! *All* of it will be yours in abundance when that day comes.

Lord, I'm looking forward to heaven, not just to feast my eyes on the delights to come, but to see You face-to-face and experience Your glory in ways I can only imagine! How I praise You, Lord! Amen.

More Transformation

Do not conform to the pattern of this world, but be transformed by the renewing of your mind. Then you will be able to test and approve what God's will is—his good, pleasing and perfect will.

ROMANS 12:2 NIV

Change is hard. In fact, it's so difficult that we often resist it. But true and lasting change (what we would call "transformation") is totally worth the effort.

Maybe you've already transformed. You've changed your thinking about something. You've shifted your attitude. And you're seeing the world differently now.

God designed you to appreciate and adapt to change. He created you for transformation. And He's not just interested in seeing your political opinions change or your culinary tastes adapt. He's looking for long and lasting change—change that morphs you into His image.

Yes, you were designed to transform into the image (or likeness) of God!

"How is that possible?" you ask. To be more like Him, you need to spend more time with Him. (It's a proven fact that we become more like the ones we hang out with, after all.)

Don't conform to the world; be transformed into Christ's image. Change your mind. Make it more like His.

I want to be more like You, Jesus! Help me in every area of my life, I pray. Amen.

More Self-Control

But the fruit of the Spirit is love, joy, peace, patience, kindness,
goodness, faithfulness, gentleness, self-control;
against such things there is no law.
GALATIANS 5:22-23 ESV

"I can say no to that."

Alyssa stood in front of the open freezer door, staring at the carton of ice cream inside. It beckoned her, like a lighthouse drawing her safely to shore. Oh, how she wanted it. She could almost taste the yummy chocolate chips now.

"No." She shook her head as she closed the freezer door. "I'm saying no to that."

Saying no isn't easy, but sometimes it's the best thing we can do. And before you say, "Oh man! I have such a hard time saying no—to things, people, and so on," hold up a minute. You are empowered by the King of all kings! He has given you His Spirit and all of the gifts attached. Self-control is one of those gifts!

You were made to exhibit more self-control—whether you think you can or not.

Oh, and by the way, you can! (And you should!)

Lord, thank You for the reminder that I can do all things through
You—even say no! Thanks for gifting me self-control. Amen.

More Time Suited Up

*Put on the full armor of God, so that you can
take your stand against the devil's schemes.*
EPHESIANS 6:11 NIV

Maybe you know that feeling—being attacked by someone completely out of the blue. Later, as you describe the event, you say things like, "I never saw that one coming!" or "I didn't even know she was mad at me! I was so shocked when she went off on me!" There's just no way to process it, because the situation makes no sense to you.

Life is filled with battles, and many of them (illnesses, wars, broken friendships) come from seemingly out of nowhere, just like that. They make no sense at all. That's why it's so important to be suited up in God's armor. He has a plan to protect you from the enemy, and you were created to be armed at all times.

So dress yourself each morning. Put on the breastplate of righteousness, the shoes of peace, and the rest of your battle gear. Then, when unexpected hits come—and they will—you will be ready!

*Lord, I want to be well prepared so that I'm completely protected
at all times. I don't know when the enemy will strike, but he won't
knock me down if I'm suited up and ready for battle! Amen.*

More Praise

*Why, my soul, are you downcast? Why so disturbed
within me? Put your hope in God, for I will yet
praise him, my Savior and my God.*

PSALM 42:11 NIV

You're going through a distressing time, and everyone who knows you can see it. You couldn't hide it if you tried, nor would your loved ones want you to. You've earned the right to cry, to mourn. And so you do. You give yourself over to the pain of it all, ready to be depleted through your tears and groanings.

And then a gentle nudge from the Holy Spirit reminds you that you were created for more than the pain. You were designed to praise—even in the middle of the darkest situations. No, it doesn't make sense. But, yes, it feels so right.

So you lift your head. You tilt your face toward heaven and cry out, "I praise You, Father!" in the very midst of the battle. Others might think you've lost your mind, but you don't care. Praising your way through the storm is the only way to go.

The pain doesn't go away—at least not completely. But over time, as you praise your way through, it begins to fade away. And the power that comes from praise invigorates you to keep going, no matter how rocky the path in front of you.

*Lord, I praise You today. Things in my life aren't perfect.
I'm facing problems galore. But that won't stop my praise.
I'll power my way through with Your help, Father! Amen.*

More Strength to Get the Job Done

And let us not grow weary of doing good,
for in due season we will reap, if we do not give up.
GALATIANS 6:9 ESV

Katherine was great at starting things—just not so great at finishing them. All you had to do was take a peek at the half-painted kitchen to figure that out. Or the scrapbook she'd started. Or the Bible study she joined but never attended. Starting was easy. Staying on top of things, not so much. She always seemed to lose interest and then move on to the next thing.

Maybe you can relate. You dive into a project with gusto but feel yourself zapped of interest a short while later. If so, there's great news for you today: God has created you for more strength to finish those tasks. It's true! You will reap a harvest in due season if you don't give up.

So don't quit. Dust yourself off, and then dig back in to that half-done project. Pray. Ask God to give you all you need. You were made to finish, and you'll be so glad you did!

Lord, I want to be known as a woman who finishes well. I don't
want to quit halfway. Give me the strength and tenacity to
finish the tasks You place in front of me, Father. Amen.

More Self-Discipline

*For the Spirit God gave us does not make us timid,
but gives us power, love and self-discipline.*
2 TIMOTHY 1:7 NIV

What does it mean to have self-discipline? Do you need a daily chart with "Do this, don't do that" written down? (Maybe! Some people do better with lists, after all.) Most of us simply need to learn to say no to our own desires. That last slice of chocolate cake? Give it to your hubby. That dress you're dying to buy? Skip it. Those new shoes? C'mon now. Do you really need another pair?

Temptations abound, but God made you to be disciplined. It will feel so good when you're able to sponsor that child in a third world country or contribute to your church's food bank instead of buying something new for yourself. And that's the truth! God designed you to be generous, and that's not possible if you spend all of your resources on things you don't really need.

Here's an important question you can ask yourself when you're facing any sort of temptation: "Do I *really* need that?" If the answer is no, then skip it!

*Thanks for reminding me that I can skip it if I don't really
need it, Lord. I want to be more self-disciplined. Amen.*

More Confidence in Him, Not You

*Let us then approach God's throne of grace with
confidence, so that we may receive mercy and
find grace to help us in our time of need.*
HEBREWS 4:16 NIV

"Square those shoulders! Stand up straight!"

Elisa replayed her mother's words in her mind time and time again. Years had passed, but those stern messages remained.

"Act like you're confident even if you're not!"

And Elisa tried. Oh, she tried. But pretending to be confident required, well, confidence.

Maybe you were raised with similar admonitions. You struggled with confidence from early childhood like Elisa, perhaps. But God wants you to know that He designed you to be confident—not in your own abilities, but in His. You don't have to fake it. You don't have to pretend. (You probably do yourself more harm when you're acting.) Instead, seek the real deal in Jesus Christ.

*Confidence is only found in You, Lord! I want the real deal,
not the cheater's version. No more faking it till I make it.
I'll never make it without You, Father. Amen.*

More Transcendent Peace

And the peace of God, which transcends all understanding,
will guard your hearts and your minds in Christ Jesus.
PHILIPPIANS 4:7 NIV

God's peace doesn't just defy understanding; it sails above and beyond anything we could ask or think. Our finite minds can't fully comprehend the things of God. The peace He provides often surprises us when we least expect it.

Like right in the middle of a crisis. Or sitting at the bedside of a dying loved one. Or facing a proverbial giant. Even in those very difficult circumstances, God offers peace that floods our hearts and prevents us from giving up. We don't have to hype ourselves up to receive it. We don't have to work hard to keep it. It simply wraps itself around us like a warm blanket on a cold day. And as soon as it takes hold, we're remedied. Peace changes *everything*.

Are you in need of God's supernatural peace today? You were designed to receive it. Open your heart and mind to the truth of His Word, and then watch as He bathes you in peace that passes all understanding.

Lord, I need Your peace today.
May it guard my heart and my mind. Amen.

More Joy

The LORD is my strength and shield. I trust him with
all my heart. He helps me, and my heart is filled
with joy. I burst out in songs of thanksgiving.

PSALM 28:7 NLT

As a child, you probably sang about joy. You had the "joy, joy, joy, joy down in your heart!" No doubt, childish giggles followed the singing of the song. You simply couldn't help yourself.

These days the joy isn't always as easy to find (or to sing about). Life has intervened. Bills require your attention. Kids squabble with one another. Your spouse can't find the papers you need for the mortgage company. And there you are in the middle of it all, trying to hold everything together. (Not much joy in that, is there?)

But maybe there is! God created you for more joy! More in the bad times, more in the good. More in the chaos, more in the pain. More in the upswing, more in the down.

Joy is an energy booster. It is God's gift to you—a bubbling, untroubling present that lifts your spirits on seemingly unliftable days.

God designed you to have the joy, joy, joy, joy, girl. So let it flow!

Lord, I'm here, arms uplifted,
ready to receive Your joy! Amen.

More Sacrifice

And so, dear brothers and sisters, I plead with you to give
your bodies to God because of all he has done for you.
Let them be a living and holy sacrifice—the kind he will
find acceptable. This is truly the way to worship him.
<small>ROMANS 12:1 NLT</small>

Sacrifice sounds like a dirty word, doesn't it? To sacrifice something means that you give it up. But what if you don't want to? Life is filled with many instances of giving up things we don't want to give, after all.

But God's views on sacrifice are far different; He views our sacrifices as gifts. That time you spent baking cookies for the elderly neighbor? A lovely sacrifice. The money you gave up so that your loved one could have what they needed? A beautiful gift.

You were designed to sacrifice—everything from your time to your finances—and all in service to the Lord. He's not stealing anything from you. On the contrary, He offers timely opportunities to give, because giving (*sacrificing*) grows you into a precious, selfless woman of God.

Lord, I can't believe I'm saying this, but I want to sacrifice more!
When the ideas are Yours, not mine, You make provision. You have
a lovely plan. So show me how and where to give, Father. Amen.

More Captivity of Thoughts

We demolish arguments and every pretension that sets itself up against the knowledge of God, and we take captive every thought to make it obedient to Christ.

2 Corinthians 10:5 NIV

The hunter set his trap—a mound of ropes twisted and tied, then fastened to a tree. The cougar moved with stealthy steps across the forest floor, unaware of the trap set before him—until he was already in its grips. The ropes tightened and pulled, and he was suspended midair.

Why would God ask us to take our thoughts captive like a wild beast caught in a trap? What is He trying to tell us?

You were designed to have control over your thoughts, not have your thoughts take control over you. Your thoughts can't be allowed to dominate, or you will end up trapped like that cougar—not by ropes but by vain imaginings. You'll be so twisted up in your thinking that you won't be able to function normally.

God didn't design you to be caught in that trap, sister; He designed you to take your thoughts captive so that you can, once and for all, be free.

I get it, Lord! I won't be trapped. Instead, I'll trap my thoughts. And in doing so, I'll be set free! Amen.

More Protection

Though a thousand fall at your side, though ten thousand
are dying around you, these evils will not touch you.
PSALM 91:7 NLT

Picture this: the battle is hot and heavy, and soldiers are dropping all around you. There you stand, watching them fall and wondering if you're going to survive. Your knees knock. You are overcome with fear. What should you do?

Fear is not from the Lord. If you're facing a challenge—even the very biggest one of your life—you can still trust Him. God wants you to know that He's your protector. That doesn't only mean He'll keep the enemy off your back; it means He has your back even if you're facing a giant—like a life-threatening health diagnosis or the loss of your home.

Being protected by God doesn't mean we're immune from the challenges of this life, but it does mean that He's right there, walking through the hard times with us. He's in the fire, the flood, the illness, and the pain. His protective hand guides, directs, and comforts. And He's working out a plan for your good.

You were created for more of His covering, more of His protection. Lean on Him today no matter what you're going through. He won't let you down.

Lord, I will lean on You for protection.
With You in charge, I don't have to be afraid. Amen.

More Hope

*May the God of hope fill you with all joy and
peace in believing, so that by the power of
the Holy Spirit you may abound in hope.*

ROMANS 15:13 ESV

"Honey, you can't give up hope. You just can't."

Laura leaned her head into her hands and wept, still overcome with the news that her cancer had spread. How could her husband ask her not to give up now, with the PET scan clearly showing things were getting worse, not better? Couldn't he see that her battle was coming to an end? How dare he try to fill her with hope at a time like this! Surely he saw the gravity of the situation.

Hope is a priceless commodity. It's more precious than gold or diamonds. It's more valuable than all the jewels in a royal crown. Hope is what keeps us going when everything around us screams, *Just give up already!*

Hope is what we need when we don't know what we need. It's a propellant, a healer, an inspirer. And more than all of this, hope is what our heavenly Father wants us to have. We were made to be filled with hope—even in hopeless times. *Especially* in hopeless times.

*Lord, You created me to have more hope,
even in times when it makes no sense.
I place my trust in You, Almighty God! Amen.*

More Than Your Heartache

The LORD is close to the brokenhearted;
he rescues those whose spirits are crushed.
PSALM 34:18 NLT

Anita's husband passed away unexpectedly. One morning he simply didn't wake up. Anita was in a state of shock, and so were her grown children. How could such a thing happen?

The following weeks and months were a blur. She somehow made it through the funeral and the liquidation of his business. But when she discovered their finances weren't as solid as her husband had led her to believe, the pain hit all over again—but this time it was a different sort of pain.

Maybe you've been through real heartache like Anita's. Perhaps you've lost someone you love or lost a business or been through the tragedy of a catastrophic storm.

Life will break your heart time and time again. But God doesn't want the pain to last forever. You are more than your heartache. And God has good things planned for you on the other side of the tragedy. Trust Him today even if you haven't in days past. Put your hand back in His and trust that He's going to take care of you from this day forward.

Lord, I trust You, even in my pain. Amen.

More Victories

You will walk upon the lion and the snake. You will crush under your feet the young lion and the snake.
PSALM 91:13 NLV

A TV preacher hollers, "You're a winner! You have the victory!" and we cringe. Perhaps it's not the words but the preacher's delivery that causes us to doubt the overall message. Maybe we get the idea that victory comes from us rather than from God.

The preacher is right in saying that we were created to be victorious. Just keep in mind that the power to triumph comes from just one place—Jesus Christ. Does this mean you'll win every single battle or come out on top in every situation? Absolutely not! However, you'll learn more from your losses than your gains, and character is formed in times of loss.

But don't give up on being victorious just because the message has been overplayed. God wants you to triumph over sin. He wants you to triumph over addiction. He longs for you to triumph in your relationships. And He's standing right there, loaded with the power to help you come through all of your hardships.

You were made to be victorious, girl! Don't give up now!

I am a victor in You, Lord! Thanks for giving me the courage to triumph. Amen.

More Alert

Be alert and of sober mind. Your enemy the devil prowls around like a roaring lion looking for someone to devour.
1 PETER 5:8 NIV

Celia was one of those girls who had a hard time falling asleep at night—as a result, mornings were torture. When the alarm went off, she would awaken, but not completely. A ten-minute snooze didn't do much to make her feel like getting up, but at that point she had no choice. There were bills to pay, after all, so off to work she went—day in and day out. And though she was showered, dressed, and seated behind her desk an hour later, Celia still didn't feel fully awake. Yawns overtook her as the morning progressed.

Maybe you're like Celia—you're just not a morning person. And by the time you get to work, you're still not fully present. It's one thing to live like that in the physical but another altogether to doze off spiritually speaking. God designed you to be fully awake, sister! No falling asleep on the job for you! There's a very real enemy out there, and he would love nothing more than to take you down. So stay alert. Keep your eyes wide open. You have big tasks ahead of you, and they require you to be fully engaged.

Lord, I won't doze off and let the enemy catch me off guard. I'll be alert and ready, fully engaged. Amen.

More Powerful Prayers

Therefore confess your sins to each other and pray for
each other so that you may be healed. The prayer
of a righteous person is powerful and effective.

JAMES 5:16 NIV

It's one thing to have a quick chat with an acquaintance in the grocery store; it's another thing to sit down over a cup of coffee with your best friend and spill your guts.

Jesus is a "spill your guts" kind of friend. He wants more coffee time with you. He doesn't just want you to spout the usual, "Bless my kids, and thanks for my job" prayers. He's looking for you to get to the deep stuff—like how you're feeling after you lost the promotion at work, or what made you snap at the kids yesterday morning as they left for school. He wants to listen to all of it, and then He'll respond, wrapping His arms of love around you in the process.

Powerful prayers should be part of your DNA. God created you to communicate with Him. So don't just scratch the surface; commit to a genuine encounter with Him every time you pray.

Lord, sometimes I feel like I need Your guidance to
know how to pray effectively. Teach me how
so that I can go deep with You. Amen.

More Help in Time of Trouble

God is our refuge and strength,
an ever-present help in trouble.

PSALM 46:1 NIV

Growing up, Melanie was the one always giving help, not the one receiving. The oldest of six children, she was usually changing diapers, feeding the little ones, or trying to help her mother out with meals. When she needed help with homework, she rarely received it. When she had a problem with a friend at school, there was rarely anyone to talk it over with.

Maybe you've been in Melanie's shoes; you were always the giver and rarely the receiver of help. If so, there's good news for you today. God created you to receive help in times of trouble. Even when no one around you seems to notice what's going on, He does. He sees, He cares, and He's ready to intervene. So reach out to Him today. Watch as He pours out His abiding love and concern over your situation. And don't be surprised when He begins to move heaven and earth on your behalf. That's how much He adores you, sister!

Thank You for being my help in times of trouble, Lord.
You are my refuge and my strength, and I'm so grateful! Amen.

More Glory

*For I consider that the sufferings of this present
time are not worth comparing with the
glory that is to be revealed to us.*

ROMANS 8:18 ESV

Have you ever looked at something through a filter? Maybe you've applied a filter to a photo of yourself and it changed everything. Gone were the wrinkles, the blemishes, the double chin. The filter took care of all of it, and you could pass as a model!

Did you know that God has a filter that He wants you to view all of life through? It's His "glory filter." His glory has been revealed to us, and it changes (literally!) *everything*. The pain of a loved one's death? Changed when you glimpse it through the glory veil. The agony of losing a job? Eased when viewed through His glory.

When we gain an eternal perspective—when we see all of life through the lens of eternity—how our perspective shifts! Suddenly the troubles of this life are minuscule in comparison to the joy that is to come.

You were created for more glory, girl! Put that filter in place and see how the world changes!

*My sufferings cannot compare, Lord,
to the glory of Your presence. Thank You
for giving me an eternal perspective. Amen.*

More Seasons of Refreshing

*He refreshes my soul. He guides me
along the right paths for his name's sake.*
PSALM 23:3 NIV

Work, work, work. It felt like that was all Kathleen ever did. Whether she was at her office or standing over a sink full of dirty dishes, work beckoned. Laundry for the family, paperwork for the boss—her work never seemed to end.

But then her husband surprised her with a gift—she and her best friend would have three glorious days at a resort in Galveston. Kathleen could hardly believe it. She packed her bags, met up with her friend, and off they went. They spent the days laughing, eating, swimming, and sleeping. In between it all, they had the sweetest conversations about all the Lord was doing in their lives. Before their time together came to an end, they prayed for each other and committed to keep those prayers coming, even after they were back at home.

Seasons of refreshing are God's plan for you, sister. He doesn't like to see you burned out or exhausted. Look for opportunities to rest and refresh as often as you can.

*Thank You for seasons of refreshing,
Lord! How I need them! Amen.*

More Answers from On High

*He will call on me, and I will answer him; I will be
with him in trouble, I will deliver him and honor him.*

PSALM 91:15 NIV

For hours Sharen tried to reach her boyfriend on the phone. He didn't answer. She tried texting, but her messages went unanswered too. By day's end, she was genuinely worried. Why would he avoid her like this?

The next morning, she received a call from him. The day before, he had dropped his phone in the kitchen sink (which just happened to be full of water!), and his phone was ruined. Fortunately, he was able to replace his phone quickly.

Maybe you've been there. You've lost your ability to communicate because your phone died. Or maybe you've been on the other end—you were the one making calls that went unanswered.

Here's a delightful truth: God will *always* answer when you call. His phone is never out of service. He's prompt too. You call and He answers! Just like that. And you can expect Him to continue doing what He has promised. He will respond because He adores you.

*I'm so glad You answer when I call, Lord.
You'll never leave me hanging. Amen.*

More Work for Him

I have been crucified with Christ and I no longer live,
but Christ lives in me. The life I now live in the body, I live by
faith in the Son of God, who loved me and gave himself for me.
GALATIANS 2:20 NIV

In the late 1960s Frank Sinatra popularized a song you've probably heard titled "My Way." In it he sings the praises of having lived life his own way, not caring about the impact on others. We all tend to want things our way; but once you ask Jesus to live in your heart, it's *His* way, not yours.

So how can you transition your thinking to be more about the work you do *for Him* than the pleasure you take for yourself? The answer is found in Galatians 2:20. You've been crucified; every part of you has been put to death and then resurrected to be more like Him. He now lives in you. He guides, directs, invigorates. He breathes through you, His Spirit propelling you to do more, be more, love more, care more—all so that others might come to know Him.

The kind of work God calls you to is more fun and adventurous than anything you could have dreamed for yourself. Do it for Him—the Love of your life.

I'm ready to work hard for You, my Savior and King. Amen.

More Exaltation

He says, "Be still, and know that I am God; I will be exalted among the nations, I will be exalted in the earth."
PSALM 46:10 NIV

Society elevates all sorts of people—from movie stars to musicians to sports heroes. We see their faces plastered on magazine covers, in articles on the internet, and on entertainment TV shows. When one of them gets married or has a baby, the whole world knows about it—*every tiny detail*. They consume our conversations and our thoughts. We take a vested interest, as if they were family members.

There is One who is exalted above all people, places, and things. He's greater than any movie star, more talented than the finest musician, and stronger than any athlete. His name is Jesus Christ, and He *alone* deserves your full adoration and exaltation. If anyone should have your full attention and interest, it should be Him!

You were created to spend more time exalting your Lord and Savior. He is worthy of your praise. He saved you, sanctified you, and gave you eternal life, after all. (Bet you can't name one movie star who even comes close.)

*Lord, I exalt You! Above all people—famous or infamous—
You reign! There is none like You, Jesus. Amen.*

More Healing by His Wounds

But he was pierced for our transgressions, he was crushed
for our iniquities; the punishment that brought us peace
was on him, and by his wounds we are healed.

ISAIAH 53:5 NIV

What a sobering verse from the book of Isaiah!

Jesus' death was all for us. Even the torture He endured before the moment of death was for us. He was pierced (in His side with a sword) for our transgressions. It's almost too much to take in, isn't it? He was literally "crushed for our iniquities."

Because of me, Lord? You went through that torture because of
Your great love for me?

And then the most beautiful part of all: "the punishment that brought us peace was on him, and by his wounds we are healed."

Think about that for a moment—let it sink deep into your soul. If Jesus hadn't gone to the cross—if He had said, "Thanks, but I don't think so," to God's plan for redemption—we never would have been healed spiritually, emotionally, physically, or mentally. We would be broken, irreparable, if He hadn't followed through with God's plan!

Thankfully we'll never have to worry about that. Jesus took care of absolutely everything.

Thank You, Lord, for the healing that
has come from Your wounds. Amen.

More Grace

But he said to me, "My grace is sufficient for you,
for my power is made perfect in weakness."
2 CORINTHIANS 12:9 ESV

Brianna was always too hard on herself. If she made a mistake, she beat herself up over it. If she cooked a meal, it was never good enough. If she posted on social media, she would question every single word. Her hair wasn't as stylish as her friends'; her body was too lumpy; she didn't see herself as being either witty or charming.

At some point in her childhood, Brianna's father withdrew all grace and treated her harshly. Consequently, this became a learned behavior. If her father didn't think she was worthy of grace, then she wouldn't either.

And it didn't stop with only herself. Brianna had a hard time extending grace to others as well. She couldn't seem to help herself.

Maybe Brianna's story is hitting a nerve. Maybe it's a little too close to home. You were made to receive and give more and more grace, sister. So don't beat yourself up! God created you for more than that!

I will do my best not to be so hard on myself (and others),
Lord, but I'm going to need Your help. Amen.

More Separation of Light from Darkness

And God saw that the light was good.
And God separated the light from the darkness.

GENESIS 1:4 ESV

"You can't straddle the fence, honey."

Sarah looked into her mother's eyes. "What do you mean, Mom?"

"You need to make up your mind. You can't spend half your time partying with your friends and the other half saying you're a Christian. I'm not saying you should walk away from friendships, but I am saying that more space is called for if you're trying to be different from the rest of the pack."

Maybe you can relate to Sarah's struggle. You love hanging out with your friends—even the ones who are far from God. They're so much fun. Okay, they do a lot of things they shouldn't, but you overlook their shortcomings. "No judging" and all that. Right?

It's one thing to maintain a friendship with someone who is in the dark; it's another to align yourself with her. It's time to separate the light from darkness, girl. How will you ever grow in your relationship with the Lord if you spend so much time partying in the dark?

Lord, the decision is made. I'm separating light
from darkness once and for all. I choose light! Amen.

More of His Understanding

Trust in the LORD with all your heart,
and do not lean on your own understanding.
PROVERBS 3:5 ESV

How many times have you said in frustration, "I just can't figure this out!" Maybe you were trying to figure out why a friend suddenly quit speaking to you. Perhaps you were trying to figure out why your paycheck didn't stretch as far this month. Or maybe you were conflicted about your child's strange behavior that seemed to crop up out of nowhere. Life is filled with opportunities to be confused, isn't it?

The hard truth is this: while it's a good thing to try to understand what's going on, there are occasions when "figuring it out" on your own isn't possible. And in those moments, all you can do is hand your confusion off to the Lord and say, "Father, You figure it out. It's beyond me."

And now for the fantastic news: He *will* handle it! He knows what's going on behind the scenes and has every answer to every question. You were designed to lean on Him—not on yourself—for understanding. Whew! Doesn't it feel good to know you don't have to do this alone? The answers aren't inside of you; they're inside of Him!

Lord, I look to You, not to myself, for answers. When it
comes to the things I can't figure out, teach me to
lean on You for understanding, Father. Amen.

More Overcoming

"I have told you these things, so that in me you may have peace. In this world you will have trouble. But take heart! I have overcome the world."

JOHN 16:33 NIV

Shelly Jo wasn't a fighter by nature. If someone came up against her, wanting to start an argument, she rarely stated her case. She would just back down instead. The same could be said of her struggles with temptation. She didn't feel like fighting, so she would just give in to the temptation. Shelly Jo didn't see herself as an overcomer; she thought of herself as a loser, which made giving in even easier.

Maybe you can relate. It's easier not to fight. It's easier just to sigh and give in. But God designed you to be an overcomer. He doesn't want you to give up without a fight. So keep going, girl! Lift your head high and keep on marching even when the enemy threatens. You *will* overcome with the heavenly Father's help!

I was made to overcome, Lord. I'm not giving in. No way, no how! In You I will take heart. Amen.

More Testifying

*Very truly I tell you, we speak of what we know,
and we testify to what we have seen, but still
you people do not accept our testimony.*
JOHN 3:11 NIV

Tiffany had suffered with migraines much of her adult life, so when she discovered a natural product that helped, she felt she had to tell people all about it. On social media she sang the praises of this product—to the point where her friends and family got a little tired of hearing it. A handful of acquaintances even unfollowed her.

Maybe you've been this excited about a product (or sports team) too. You just couldn't wait to sing its praises for all to hear. You've been guilty of filling your social media pages with glowing praises in the hopes that others would catch your enthusiasm.

Did you know that you were designed to testify? That desire to "spread the good news" is inside of you for a reason. God placed it there and desires for you to be as excited about sharing the good news about life in Jesus as you are about last night's game.

The next time you're wondering how to best share the Gospel, don't forget how fun and easy it was to share that last glowing review for your favorite restaurant, essential oil, or diet plan. Surely, if you can sing the praises of those things, you can share what God has done to change your life forever.

*Lord, give me the right words to share—whether I'm
having coffee with a close friend or posting online.
I want to testify to Your goodness! Amen.*

More Harmony

*Live in harmony with one another. Do not be
proud, but be willing to associate with people
of low position. Do not be conceited.*

Romans 12:16 NIV

Meredith was happy to attend her kid sister's choir concert—until she got there. Unfortunately, the seventh-grade girls' choir was a little off pitch. Okay, more than a little. They were just plain awful.

Meredith, a consummate musician, thought she might lose her mind as several of the sopranos screeched out a note that didn't even come close to what they were aiming for. The whole thing was reminiscent of fingernails on a chalkboard. *Eek!*

Harmony is lovely but only when it works. If the sopranos, altos, tenors, and basses don't sing in the same key, the song is doomed.

The same is true when relationships aren't harmonious. When people begin to squabble or cause unnecessary friction, the whole dynamic can change (and not for the better). God never intended for us to fall out of harmony with friends, family members, coworkers, or loved ones. He longs for us to love the way He loves and for harmony to flow. So tuck away any pride, and do your best to get along. No fingernails down the proverbial chalkboard for you!

*Lord, I want harmonious relationships. Thank You for showing
me that it is possible, even with difficult people. Amen.*

More Delight in His Law

*Blessed is the man who walks not in the counsel of the
wicked, nor stands in the way of sinners, nor sits in the
seat of scoffers; but his delight is in the law of the LORD,
and on his law he meditates day and night.*

PSALM 1:1–2 ESV

Following the rules wasn't Linda's thing. In fact, she spent most of her life trying to figure out how to avoid them. By the time she reached adulthood, little things—like being honest with her boss about why she was late to work—were easier to lie about. Before long few people believed anything she said, but she didn't really care. Rules just weren't for her.

Maybe you can relate to Linda. You don't like to be told what to do. You don't care for the confines of rules. They irritate you. They feel intrusive.

Try to picture life without rules for a moment. What if there was no speed limit? What if alcohol could be consumed at any age? What if you didn't have to wait until adulthood to be in the military? What if you could take whatever you wanted from any store?

Chaos reigns without rules, and eventually it took over Linda's life. But you were made for more than all that. God created you to live in peace and harmony, and the only way for that to happen is by following His plan for order in your life.

*Lord, I choose to follow Your commands because I
know they will bring life and health to my soul! Amen.*

More Shining Like the Sun

*"Then the righteous will shine like the sun in the kingdom
of their Father. Whoever has ears, let them hear."*

MATTHEW 13:43 NIV

Remember that song you used to sing as a kid about not hiding your light under a bushel? You were born to let the light of God shine bright—in your actions, your words, and your attitude.

Maybe you hear that and say, "But you don't know the valley I'm walking through right now. How can I possibly shine my light? There's just no way."

People are watching *right now*. They want hope. And they're waiting for someone in the valley to pipe up and say, "Hey, guys! I'm here too, but I'm not giving up on Jesus! I'm not letting go of my faith."

Be the light. *Shine* the light. Don't be afraid to speak up, especially in hard times. So what if you slip up one day and come back shining the next? Others won't see you as a hypocrite; you'll just look like what you are—human.

*Lord, I want to shine like the sun! I'll mess up from
time to time and accidentally let my light go out.
But I'll be back to shining with Your help, Father. Amen.*

More Caring for the Downtrodden

*Do nothing out of selfish ambition or vain conceit. Rather,
in humility value others above yourselves, not looking to your
own interests but each of you to the interests of the others.*
PHILIPPIANS 2:3–4 NIV

Patti just couldn't stop herself. Her heart went out to those less fortunate, and she had to help. The homeless man at the busy intersection? She made sure to keep bottled water and pop-top cans of tuna in her car for him. The local women's shelter? She volunteered to serve food every Thanksgiving. Her church's food pantry? She did her best to keep it stocked. Patti simply couldn't live with the notion that people in unfortunate situations wouldn't receive the things they needed.

Maybe you're a little bit like Patti; it breaks your heart to see people in genuine need. Maybe you're the one buying Christmas gifts for underprivileged children or baking pumpkin pies for the shelter's holiday gathering.

God created you to care about those less fortunate. Every ounce of passion that's stirring inside of you is straight from His heart. So do what you can, sister! Look to the interests of others, and you'll never go wrong.

*Lord, thank You for the reminder that You created me to
care about those less fortunate than myself. I want to
do all I can, Father. Thank You for Your help. Amen.*

More Confidence to Draw Near

Let us then with confidence draw near to the throne of grace, that we may receive mercy and find grace to help in time of need.

HEBREWS 4:16 ESV

Jasmine adopted a dog from a local shelter. He was the sweetest little thing—an eight-month-old retriever mix weighing in at twenty-nine pounds. She didn't know much about the pooch's background, but one thing was evident—he had clearly suffered some sort of abuse. This was clear every time she reached out to touch him. He would duck his head and lower his body like he was expecting her to harm him.

It took several weeks of letting him know he was safe before the sweet dog finally came around. He ended up being her sidekick, the perfect, confident companion.

Maybe you've spent a few years cowering too. You've not trusted God to treat you well. You think He'll be as cruel as some of the people you've known in your past. But God adores you. He's the perfect Master, one you can trust—totally, fully, and completely. So don't be afraid to draw near. He longs to spend time with you.

Lord, today I choose to draw near to You. I want to know You more. You are a good, good Father. Amen.

More Increase

May the LORD give you increase,
you and your children!
PSALM 115:14 ESV

Jenny grew up in a family that lived on the edge of poverty. Her father was a kind man but not a hard worker. He didn't seem to be a huge fan of any job he tried and consequently ended up losing most of them.

Her mother was frustrated with the situation but didn't know what to do to change it, short of babysitting the neighbor's little girl for a bit of cash. So they muddled along, barely making ends meet year after year.

Maybe you've been in the same boat and you wonder if things will ever change. You read the words, "May the LORD give you increase" and secretly wonder if that's even a possibility.

God longs to meet your needs—and also surprise you with His blessings. You will have tasks to complete along the way, but He has a job that is perfect for you, a decent paycheck, and a few added blessings too. So trust the heavenly Father with your finances.

Lord, I'm done with worrying about financial matters.
I know You long to bless me above all I could ask or
think. I trust You for the increase, Father. Amen.

More Faithfulness in Giving

"Bring the full tithe into the storehouse, that there may be
food in my house. And thereby put me to the test, says the
LORD of hosts, if I will not open the windows of heaven for you
and pour down for you a blessing until there is no more need."
MALACHI 3:10 ESV

It's impossible to outgive God. No matter how much you give—of your time, talents, or treasures—He *always* returns it multiplied back to you.

Maybe you've struggled with this whole "giving to God" thing. You say things like, "Why does God need my money anyway? Doesn't He already own the cattle on a thousand hills?"

He does, but He's testing you to see if you trust Him. And lest you think that money you're giving to the local church is being frittered away, think again. There are salaries and utility bills to be paid, mission organizations to fund, and local families to feed. Your portion goes a long way in making all that possible.

Be faithful with your giving. God will bless you in ways you never saw coming.

Lord, I give out of great love—for Your church, Your people,
and Your plan for my life. I trust You, Father. Amen.

More Power from the Holy Spirit

"But you will receive power when the Holy Spirit has come upon you, and you will be my witnesses in Jerusalem and in all Judea and Samaria, and to the end of the earth."

ACTS 1:8 ESV

Judy felt like her battery was only half charged much of the time. The problem wasn't just physical exhaustion; it was the emotional baggage she carried from years past. She watched others—her coworkers, neighbors, and friends—move with ease and grace through life and wondered if she would ever reach that point herself.

The Judys of this world struggle with feelings of depletion. They feel powerless and overwhelmed. Perhaps you've felt that way at times too. You didn't have the energy to get out of bed in the morning, put on clothes, and go to work.

God made you for more than that, sister! He gives you the physical energy you need to keep going, but even more important, He fills You with His Spirit so you can do great things for God's kingdom.

Not feeling it at the moment? Ask for an infilling today. Then get ready! God's going to charge your battery like never before!

Lord, today I ask for You to fill me to overflowing with Your power! Amen.

More Purpose for Each Day

*God's purpose in all this was to use the church to display
his wisdom in its rich variety to all the unseen rulers and
authorities in the heavenly places. This was his eternal
plan, which he carried out through Christ Jesus our Lord.*

EPHESIANS 3:10–11 NLT

What if you faced every moment of every day with a sense of purpose and drive? What if you woke up in the morning and asked God this question: "Where are You taking me today?" and then fully expected Him to lead you there?

Wouldn't life change for the better if you felt driven by the notion that the almighty Author of all had a plan and a purpose for each day of your life?

Maybe today you're supposed to let a single mom pour out her heart while you offer comfort and calm. Perhaps this is the day that you're supposed to pick up the tab for the older gentleman at the coffee shop. Maybe you'll discover this is the day you meet someone who is going to be a part of your life for years to come.

Trusting God with all the moments is key. Stepping out in faith also plays a role. But understanding that the Lord has a purpose—not just in the general sense, but every single day—that's the motivator!

*Lord, where are You taking me today?
I'm ready to go! Amen.*

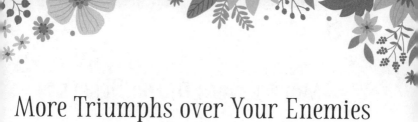

More Triumphs over Your Enemies

The LORD is on my side as my helper;
I shall look in triumph on those who hate me.

PSALM 118:7 ESV

Jenna couldn't seem to shake the woman at work who—for whatever reason—seemed to despise her. This woman would do anything and everything to make Jenna look bad, especially in front of the boss. She tried to fight back (or to catch the woman in the act), but this woman was clever. She seemed to have a knack for making herself look good and others look bad.

Maybe you've been through something like this. An unexpected enemy rose up and did what he or she could to defeat you, and you were unaware the attack was coming.

Did you know that God has a plan for your enemies? It's true! You were created to triumph over them. Does that mean every nasty person will automatically disappear from your life (or get caught in the act of hurting you)? Nope. Sometimes the story will twist and turn a bit. But in the end, in whatever way He chooses to handle it, God will cause you to triumph.

Lord, I know You have my back. I trust You to guide
me safely past any who seek to harm me. Amen.

More Rivers in the Desert

"Remember not the former things, nor consider the things of old. Behold, I am doing a new thing; now it springs forth, do you not perceive it? I will make a way in the wilderness and rivers in the desert."

ISAIAH 43:18–19 ESV

Picture a herd of deer in a field. They romp and play. Together they chase off an incoming predator. And when the midday sun hovers overhead, bringing heat, they get thirsty. Together they travel to get a drink. The water isn't nearby, but they've learned the way—just past the clump of trees, beyond the hill, and over the rocky cliff. There lies a clear stream, its waters flowing over rocks as it moves swiftly along. The deer drink until they are satisfied, their thirst now a thing of the past.

Dear one, God created you for more times at His river of refreshing. He doesn't want you to wait until you're fully parched to head His way. The Lord wants you to learn the truth—that daily times of refreshing will keep you healthy and content in Him.

What are you thirsting for today? What has caused you to become parched and dry? Head to the river and wait in hopeful expectation as God replenishes your soul and gives you all you need for the journey.

I was made for more time at the river with You, Lord.
Thank You for meeting me there. Amen.

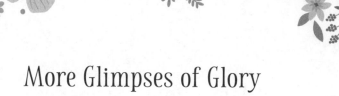

More Glimpses of Glory

The Word became flesh and dwelt among us,
and we have seen his glory, glory as of the only
Son from the Father, full of grace and truth.

JOHN 1:14 ESV

It's impossible to have an encounter with God and walk away unchanged. To step into His presence, to experience His glory, is something you'll never forget. Like Moses on the mountaintop with God, your entire countenance will change. People will ask, "What happened to you?"

Perhaps you've encountered God in a particularly powerful way—at a women's retreat, in a church service, or maybe in your own living room. His presence is sweet, powerful, and timely. How precious. How refreshing!

The Word became flesh. Ponder that for a moment. Jesus became flesh and dwelt among us, and because of this we have experienced His glory. His glory is overwhelming to us (as it should be). One day, when we're all in heaven together, we'll experience that glory as never before. Oh, what a day that will be!

Lord, thank You for the glimpses of glory I've had
here on earth. I can hardly wait for heaven,
where I will dwell with You forever! Amen.

More Roots Deepened

*I pray that out of his glorious riches he may strengthen you
with power through his Spirit in your inner being, so that
Christ may dwell in your hearts through faith. And I pray
that you [may be] rooted and established in love.*

EPHESIANS 3:16–17 NIV

The most beautiful oak tree shaded Natasha's front yard, but over time it caused unexpected problems. The tree's roots were shallow and bumpy. They impeded the growth of grass and provided a danger for lawn mower blades. Before long she couldn't even walk across the lawn without tripping. If only the tree roots had traveled downward instead of outward.

There's a reason God wants our roots to go down deep. When we're not deeply rooted, any type of storm can come along and topple us. A broken romantic relationship? Over we go. Job loss? We trip and fall.

You were made for deep roots, girl—deeper and deeper still as you grow in your faith. Don't let the storms of life topple you. You were meant to stand strong.

*Thanks for growing my roots down deep, Lord.
I want to remain upright in my faith! Amen.*

More Treasures in Heaven

"Sell your possessions, and give to the needy. Provide yourselves with moneybags that do not grow old, with a treasure in the heavens that does not fail, where no thief approaches and no moth destroys. For where your treasure is, there will your heart be also."

LUKE 12:33–34 ESV

Commercials tout it. Magazines say you can't live without *more* of it. But more of what, exactly? Money? Designer clothes? Expensive purses and jewelry? If we believed the ads that bombard us daily, we would think we deserved material possessions in excess.

The treasures this world has to offer are lovely, to be sure. Nice cars, fancy houses, expensive electronics—these things are terrific when they come our way. But they are not our true treasures.

The Bible teaches us that real treasures are laid up for us in heaven. We aren't meant to chase after material things down here on earth. And when we do have more than enough, God instructs us to remember the needy among us and to share what we have with them.

Your treasure is coming, girl. But it likely won't be in the form of a dazzling diamond or speedy sports car.

Lord, You have treasures waiting for me in heaven. I can't wait to see them! But for now I'm okay without a big mansion down here—I promise! Amen.

More Peaceful Requests

Do not be anxious about anything, but in everything
by prayer and supplication with thanksgiving
let your requests be made known to God.

PHILIPPIANS 4:6 ESV

"Just calm down, honey. Mommy can't understand what you're saying." Pam leaned down and wiped her little one's eyes.

The four-year-old gulped in air and then hollered, "I. . .I. . .I fell down and hurt my knee!"

Pam examined her daughter's knee and, sure enough, found a scrape and a bruise, which she lovingly bandaged.

Sometimes we're like that four-year-old. We come to God so worked up, so filled with emotion, that we blurt out nonsensical things to Him. In those moments, we can't see past the emotion of pain to string coherent words together.

You were designed to offer peaceful requests to the Lord—even in seasons of chaos. So, deep breath, girl. Gather your thoughts. And then make your requests known to God. He's right there and waiting to meet you at your point of need.

Lord, I'm calm. Finally! I've taken a deep breath! Now I'm ready
to come to You, emotions aside, to make my requests known.
Thank You for giving me peace in the chaos, Father. Amen.

More Help from On High

"Fear not, for I am with you; be not dismayed, for I am your God; I will strengthen you, I will help you, I will uphold you with my righteous right hand."

ISAIAH 41:10 ESV

"I need help." Tricia spoke the words, her voice quivering. She was terrified to share her situation, but she needed help and couldn't wait any longer.

She moved forward with the conversation, telling the officer about her relationship with her boyfriend. He was abusive—and not just verbally. Things had crossed a line, and she needed to get out. But she needed help to move forward.

There are moments in life when you need to trust God to get you out of precarious situations—relationships that have gone awry, jobs that are threatening your emotional health, even friendships that have become lopsided. The Lord is okay with you exiting toxic relationships, and He will be there to guide you to people who can offer assistance.

Trust the heavenly Father in the scary seasons. Keep your eyes wide open. More help is coming your way, as long as you look to Him and trust His guidance.

Lord, I come to You—for the little things and the big things too. Where else can I put my trust but in You, my Helper, my Savior, my King? Amen.

153

More Authority

*"Behold, I have given you authority to tread on
serpents and scorpions, and over all the power
of the enemy, and nothing shall hurt you."*

LUKE 10:19 ESV

Deena was growing tired of the motivational speeches. Her boss gave them all the time, and then her coworkers would get hyped up, overflowing with excitement for the tasks at hand. But they would walk out of the conference room and almost immediately return to their less-than-enthusiastic selves.

God didn't create us for hype, which never seems to last long, but for genuine victory! He has given us authority over the enemy. This means we don't need to live in defeat; we were never intended to cower and hide when faced with challenges.

What do you need to have authority over today, girlfriend? Is there a certain addiction that has you in its grip? Is there a relationship that has pinned you to the floor? Is there an area in your heart that needs healing?

You're created to exhibit authority over these things, sister. Look them in the eye and speak in the authority of Jesus' name.

*Lord, today I take authority in the name of
Jesus over the things that have held me bound! Amen.*

More Tenderhearted

*Be kind to one another, tenderhearted, forgiving
one another, as God in Christ forgave you.*
EPHESIANS 4:32 ESV

Caroline loved her job as a social worker, especially the adrenaline rush after an eventful day. When she first started her job, her heart was tender toward almost everyone she met—from the children to the single moms to the elderly. Her compassion levels were high much of the time.

But after many years in service, things began to change. She felt herself growing hard. Cold. She no longer said things like, "That poor woman! Her boyfriend abused her!" Now she shrugged and asked, "Why doesn't she just get out of the situation?" She felt her heart growing harder and wondered if it could ever soften again.

God created you to be soft and tenderhearted toward people. It's not always easy, especially when you're exposed to so much mean-spiritedness in people around you. But don't give up on the notion that the Lord created you for tenderness.

Be kind to one another. Be tenderhearted. Care about the things others care about. Sense the pain of what they're going through. It's not easy, but it's so worth it.

*Lord, give me Your tender, compassionate
heart toward everyone I meet today. Amen.*

More Resurrection Power

And God raised the Lord and will
also raise us up by his power.
1 CORINTHIANS 6:14 ESV

When you study the life of Jesus—the ups and downs, ins and outs, the healings, the relationships—do you see yourself there with Him? If so, can you imagine what the disciples were thinking and feeling on the day Jesus died on the cross? Surely, in spite of His words about rising again, many were defeated and confused.

On that morning when Jesus rose from the dead, everything changed—not just for the followers of Christ but for us today as well. When He burst forth from that tomb, the story of the Savior of the world was sealed—set in stone. He really was who He said He was! He really did what He said He would do!

The same power that propelled Jesus from the grave is alive and well inside of you today. Think about that, woman of God! The Lord created you to live, eat, sleep, and breathe in His power, not your own. Resurrection power will propel you out of any tombs you might find yourself in. Go and do great and mighty things in His power!

May I experience Your resurrection power
in all I do and say today, Lord! Amen.

More Divine Power

His divine power has given us everything we need
for a godly life through our knowledge of him who
called us by his own glory and goodness.

2 PETER 1:3 NIV

Sometimes Tessa felt like her brain didn't work properly. Oh, she made it to work on time and managed to do the daily, mundane things. But there were many times when her brain just seemed to check out. She was still there in body, but mentally she went someplace else entirely. Whenever that happened, Tessa immediately felt a sense of dread, as if she couldn't complete the task in front of her.

No doubt you've experienced this too. You're fine one minute and checked out the next, unable to complete what you've started. You were made to complete the tasks, sister! Seriously. In those moments when you're overwhelmed and completing tasks feels impossible, God grants divine (holy, heavenly) power to get things done His way.

Whew! This power sure comes in handy when you're at a standstill, frozen by fear or doubt. Supernatural power zaps you like a lightning bolt, and often when you least expect it (but most need it).

Thank You for giving me all the power
I need to get through this life, Lord! Amen.

More of His Calling

He. . .set me apart before I was born,
and. . .called me by his grace.
GALATIANS 1:15 ESV

From the time Mirabelle was a teen, she felt a call on her life to work with children. At church she volunteered in the nursery. From there she began to help out in children's church. By the time she reached her college years, Mirabelle was directing the children's ministry at her church.

Each week as she took in those precious, sweet faces of the children seated in front of her, Mirabelle's heart soared. She laughed with them, taught lessons, put together puppet shows, even led worship—all out of a heart for the kids.

Maybe you've felt a particular call on your life since childhood too. Perhaps you feel called to write. Or to act. Or to teach. Maybe you've always sensed a calling to work with homeless people or to help women in crisis.

These "calls" are God-breathed. They're not just good ideas you've drummed up. Doesn't it do your heart good to know that the Lord created and designed you to do significant things for Him? In fact, He has set you apart to do them, even before you were born. Wow! With a calling like that, how can you resist?

You've called me, Lord! Here I am,
ready to step out in faith! Amen.

More Grace and Truth

Maybe you've heard the expression "Speak the truth in love."

It's harder than it sounds, isn't it? What if the truth you need to speak is a hard truth? Your friend is asking your opinion about a task she performed poorly. Do you lie? Or do you go for it, saying something like, "Well, it wasn't your best moment."

Grace and truth came through Jesus. You might read those words and think, *What does this have to do with my friend?* Everything. He supernaturally bestows the ability to share the truth in His love. When you have to confront a child who has been disobedient, His grace can (and will) lead the way. When you've been instructed to fire an employee who continually shows up late or not at all, God can give you the grace to do so in a loving way.

Grace and truth work hand in hand. They were never meant to operate apart from one another. And Jesus Christ—the same One who offered you eternal life—offers you a way to merge grace and truth when dealing with those around you. You were made to do it, girl!

*You've given me grace for today, Lord, and I plan to use
it as needed! Thank You for sharing it with me. Amen.*

More Deliverance in Times of Trouble

When the righteous cry for help, the LORD
hears and delivers them out of all their troubles.

PSALM 34:17 ESV

Susan had a recurring dream, one she couldn't shake. In it she was walking along a path when suddenly she realized she was standing in quicksand. Though she fought valiantly to get out, she would sink deeper and deeper until she was in up to her neck. She would always wake up just as the quicksand would reach her chin.

Sometimes life is a bit like that dream You get in up to your chin and you feel like you're going under. The job. The house. The kids. The elderly parents in need of care. That is a lot to handle. But God won't let you drown. He has promised in His Word to save you. You will be delivered in times of trouble (and what a testimony when it happens).

What's pulling you under today? What has you the most weighted down? Trust God to deliver you and set your feet on solid ground. No quicksand for you, girl!

Thank You, my Deliverer, for pulling me out of the quicksand time
and time again! I'm grateful for your deliverance! Amen.

More Time Pursuing Peace

Let him turn away from evil and do good;
let him seek peace and pursue it.

1 PETER 3:11 ESV

Emma seemed to battle a never-ending undercurrent of frustration. On good days and bad it simmered like a kettle on the stove, just under the boiling point. Every now and again something—or someone—would cause it to boil over into anger. For the most part, though, she kept it tamped down as best she could.

Living with frustration can be hard. It's not something you wish for. In fact, most people wish they could get rid of it for good because it interferes with relationships and zaps the joy from so many life experiences.

How does one go about getting rid of frustration? By spending more time pursuing the peace of God. When you grab hold of His peace, you let go of anything else that's threatening to hold you back. In many ways it's like taking hold of a life raft. You have to cling to it for dear life and never let it go.

Lord, today I'm pursuing Your peace as never before.
I won't let the enemy rob me of it. It's mine for
the asking. Thank You, Father. Amen.

More Response to the Calling

*Then I heard the Lord asking, "Whom should I
send as a messenger to this people? Who will
go for us?" I said, "Here I am. Send me."*

ISAIAH 6:8 NLT

A marvelous account in the Old Testament book of Isaiah tells how
the prophet Isaiah entered God's holy presence in the temple. He was
so overcome by his own sin that he immediately felt "undone." An
angel touched Isaiah's lips with a hot coal to symbolize the removal
of his sin. Then God asked an important question: "Whom should I
send as a messenger to this people? Who will go for us?"

Without missing a beat, Isaiah said, "Here I am, Lord! Send me."

Perhaps you've experienced the call of God on your life. He has
whispered in your ear, "I want you to work with children," or "You
have a great future as a writer."

Whatever He has called you to, remember: He will equip you for
the task. So don't be afraid. And don't let the mistakes of yesterday
hold you back. You can respond with a vigorous, "Yes, Lord!" because
you are assured the glory will be His, not yours.

You were created to say yes to the call of God on your life. And
what an adventure that life will be!

Yes, Lord! I will go. Amen.

More Given Back to You

Give, and it will be given to you. A good measure, pressed down,
shaken together and running over, will be poured into your lap.
For with the measure you use, it will be measured to you.

LUKE 6:38 NIV

"Pressed down, shaken together, and running over, it will be poured into your lap."

No doubt you've heard that phrase a time or two, particularly as church offerings were being taken. It's true! No matter how much you give of your time, talents, or treasures, you can rest assured that God will return it to you with interest. Of course you don't give to get, but that doesn't change the biblical promise, does it?

The Lord has always had a plan to replenish, restore, and lavish. He's not just interested in making sure you have what you need, but in filling your vats to overflowing! So, when you give, you can expect (with confidence) that the Lord will return far more to you than what you have given. You can take that promise to the bank!

Lord, I know that more is coming my way. You astonish
me with Your generosity in my life. Thank You in
advance for meeting every need. Amen.

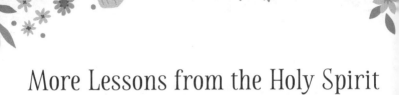

More Lessons from the Holy Spirit

"The Helper, the Holy Spirit, whom the Father will send in my name, he will teach you all things and bring to your remembrance all that I have said to you."

Life is an amazing teacher, isn't it? You eat too much, and you end up with a tummy ache. You lie to the teacher, and she doubles your workload or gives you a bad grade when you get caught. You tell Mom that your sister is the one who broke the lamp, and Mom pulls out a video showing you in the act.

Yes, there are lessons to be learned, and they don't stop when you reach adulthood. Show up late for work, and you might lose your job. Cheat on your taxes, and you go to jail.

The very best teacher of all—the one you can trust above all others—is the Holy Spirit. He can lead and guide you, teaching you all things. If you're standing at a fork in the road and don't know which way to turn, He will show you. If you're struggling to know how to respond to someone who has hurt you, the "how-to" lesson will come from the Holy Spirit if you ask Him.

I'm ready for my lessons, Lord! Thanks for being the best Teacher ever. Amen.

More Works

"Truly, truly, I say to you, whoever believes in me will also do the works that I do; and greater works than these will he do, because I am going to the Father."

JOHN 14:12 ESV

When we're young in the Lord, we say things like, "I want to do great exploits for You, Lord! Send me to Africa! Send me to the world. I'm going to do amazing things one day."

"One day" has come and gone, and no doubt you're wondering if you'll ever do anything truly magnificent for the Lord. Oh, you sponsor that child in a third world country, sure. And you put together Christmas boxes for kids in need. Yes, you contribute to your church's food pantry, but whatever happened to the "big" things you dreamed of doing?

Girl, you're doing them! Every day you pour into the lives of people around you. You minister to broken hearts by listening, you meet needs by giving, you're a diligent employee, and you pray, pray, pray. That's the very best gift of all.

You were created for greater works, so you will have more exciting adventures ahead. But until then, don't beat yourself up. You're doing amazing things for the kingdom of God!

Thanks for trusting me with greater works, Lord! Amen.

More Trusting in the Silence

"The LORD will fight for you,
and you have only to be silent."
EXODUS 14:14 ESV

She prayed for months. Then she prayed some more. But Ginger didn't get any answer at all from the Lord. Not a "wait," not a "no," not even an "I hear you." The Almighty seemed silent, and that really bothered her. Did He not care about what she was going through? After a while, she gave up praying altogether. What good was it doing?

Sometimes the Lord allows us to experience seasons of silence. No doubt you've been through them. You wonder if He is truly listening, or if He even knows you're pouring out your heart to Him.

Sweet girl, you were made to trust more in the silence. This is where your faith is sharpened. It's easy to exhibit trust when you clearly hear the Lord's voice, but when all you hear is crickets chirping, that's the most important time to hang on. When the silence is over, His voice will come breaking through loud and clear!

Lord, I choose to trust You, even in the silence.
I don't always know what You're up to, but I
continue to place my trust in You. Amen.

More Brotherly Affection

...and godliness with brotherly affection,
and brotherly affection with love.

2 PETER 1:7 ESV

Jana had a way of showing affection to others. It came across as genuine, not put on. Whenever someone was hurting—after the loss of a child, for instance, or the death of a parent—she seemed to know the right words to say to make them feel like they weren't alone. She just had a knack.

Not everyone has this gift, but it's one we should all work on. God calls us to exhibit more brotherly affection—more love and caring, not just for those in pain or need, but in general.

So, how are you in the "affection" department? Don't panic! This isn't a "hug 'em until they give up" kind of affection we're going for here, though hugs are nice. Affection can be shown with a greeting card, a text message, a hot meal, or a plate of cookies. However you choose to show it, God will honor it. So, what are you waiting for? Find someone who needs affection today!

I'll do it, Lord! I'll look for someone who is in
need of brotherly affection, and I'll pour it
out in whatever way You choose. Amen.

More Kindness toward Others

Be kind to one another, tenderhearted,
forgiving one another, as God in Christ forgave you.
EPHESIANS 4:32 ESV

"Is being kind really so hard, RaeLynn?"

The third grader looked up into her mother's eyes. It was harder than Mom knew, especially when her older brother was so mean all the time. But instead of arguing, she just sighed and did as she was told.

Maybe you've had a hard time being kind to the meanies in your life too. That boss who is so pushy. That friend who insists she knows more about everything than you. That neighbor who always has something not-so-nice to say about your yard.

Not everyone is easy to treat kindly, but that doesn't mean you shouldn't try. God created you to be kind to everyone, not just the people who make it easy.

Who is on your radar today? Who has been making life difficult? Take the kindness challenge. Go out of your way to show kindness to the very person who (in your opinion) least deserves it. Then watch and see what the Lord does.

It's not going to be easy, Lord, but I'll be kind, even to
the ones who've hurt me. I trust You in this, Father. Amen.

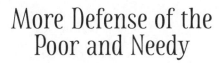

More Defense of the
Poor and Needy

*Open your mouth for the mute, for the rights of all who
are destitute. Open your mouth, judge righteously,
defend the rights of the poor and needy.*
PROVERBS 31:8-9 ESV

Brandi drove underneath the overpass every day on her way to work. She saw the men and women camped out there—some bundled in sweaters and living in cardboard boxes. How they found food, she did not know. How they kept from freezing to death in the winter, she could not say. Her heart lurched every time she saw them.

Maybe your heart breaks for those in need as well. God designed you to care about those who are less fortunate. That single mom living at the women's shelter with her two kids? Her story should touch you. That man who lost his job and can't pay the mortgage? Heartbreaking.

You were designed for more defense of the poor and needy. That's why you feel the tug to sponsor a child in a third world country. That's why you feel the familiar tug on your heart to buy groceries for that single mom. That's why you can't stay away when the elderly neighbor on a fixed income needs your help. You're touched because the heart of God is touched. And what touches Him touches you. As it should. He created you that way.

Lord, I will do what I can to help those in need. Amen.

More Adoration

Take me away with you—let us hurry! Let the king bring me into his chambers. We rejoice and delight in you; we will praise your love more than wine. How right they are to adore you!

Tasha stared into the eyes of her two-week-old son, and the tears flowed. She couldn't help it. That squishy little face. Those beautiful eyes. Those delicate lashes. She adored every single thing about her baby boy.

Adoration. That's the only word that could possibly describe how Tasha—or any new mother—feels while taking in their new baby. And God placed that feeling of adoration inside of you. He created you to adore babies, your spouse, and Him.

What does it mean to adore God? When you come into His presence and spend time with Him, a deep sense of passion fuels your time together. Perhaps the writer of Song of Songs put it best when he said, "How right they are to adore you!"

It is right to adore our marvelous Creator. Why? Because He adored us first—so much that He sent His Son as Savior for all.

Lord, I adore You! I don't care who knows! I'll sing praises to the One I adore—today and forevermore! Amen.

More Protection in Times of Trouble

The LORD is a stronghold for the oppressed,
a stronghold in times of trouble.

PSALM 9:9 ESV

Kenda's daughter, husband, and mom all came down with the flu. She went from room to room, caring for them all, dishing out meds, bowls of soup, and lots and lots of hot tea. One after the other she took temps, changed bedsheets, and even cleaned up unexpected messes. It was nothing short of a miracle that she didn't end up sick herself.

Sometimes God does that—He physically protects you in times of danger. Other times He guards your heart from things like abusive words and unkind language. The point is, God is your protector. Whether you're walking out of an abusive relationship or facing a diagnosis of cancer, He will be there to guard and protect.

The Lord has promised to be your stronghold in times of trouble. When everything else is crumbling, He won't. When everyone else is running away, He stays put. You will go through hard times—no doubt about it. But your Protector will never leave your side.

I trust You, my Protector. I'm so grateful You are
my stronghold in times of trouble, Lord! Amen.

More Family Oriented

God sets the lonely in families, he leads out the prisoners with singing; but the rebellious live in a sun-scorched land.

PSALM 68:6 NIV

They mean everything to you. Your parents, children, spouse, siblings—even those friends who are close enough to be family. You can't imagine your life without them. Sure, not every get-together is filled with family bliss, but your love binds you, even when tempers get in the way.

God designed you to operate in a family. It's where you can thrive, be encouraged, and even fail with grace sometimes.

Maybe your family unit isn't intact. Perhaps you've already lost your parents or you're single with no kiddos in the near future. God can still work in and through those you love to provide the things that families need.

Why does God care so much that you're family oriented? Because He never meant for you to go it alone. You can do more together than apart. So, get ready! He has big plans for that "unit" of yours!

Lord, thank You for my family. Please mend any broken places. Piece us together. Make us a strong unit, I pray—deepened in our faith and our love for You. Amen.

More Spirit Fruit

But the fruit of the Spirit is love, joy, peace, patience,
kindness, goodness, faithfulness, gentleness, self-control;
against such things there is no law.

GALATIANS 5:22–23 ESV

Do you ever look at the list of the fruits of the Spirit and say, "Lord, do I really have to exhibit all of them at the same time? I mean, it's hard enough to be patient, but if you throw in self-control at the same time, it's just too much."

It *is* difficult to be good all the time, isn't it? To be kind, loving, joy-filled, patient, and faithful? That hardly leaves time for hissy fits or temper tantrums. But God created you to exhibit more fruit—all at once and all of the time. No, it's not easy. Yes, you will mess this up. But God loves every step you take in the right direction.

Take a look at the list of fruits. Is there one you struggle with more than others? Does your patience wear thin? Do you have trouble remaining faithful? Give that fruit to God, and then watch as He reactivates it, making it a thing of beauty.

Lord, I give this fruit basket to You! You know my weaknesses
and strengths, Lord. Gird me up where I'm failing and help
me to be as fruity as You've called me to be. Amen.

More Giving

*Each of you should give what you have decided
in your heart to give, not reluctantly or under
compulsion, for God loves a cheerful giver.*

2 CORINTHIANS 9:7 NIV

Seasons of plenty or seasons of lack. It seems we're always in one or the other. Either we're cobbling together bits of food to call a meal or we're squandering money on eating out and shopping for a new car.

One area of our lives that should be consistent, whether we're in a season of plenty or a season of lack, is our giving. The more we love God, the more compelled we feel to give, not just when the cupboard is full, but even during the lean times too.

So, how's your giving? Do you feel led to give of your time, talents, and treasures, or are you sitting back, hoping someone else will take care of all that?

God loves a cheerful giver. And He's hoping to grow you in this area. So pull out that checkbook, girl! Get ready to give, and then watch as He uses it for His glory.

*I won't be stingy, Lord! With a heart filled with
gratitude for all You've done for me, I will give. Amen.*

More Rivers of Justice

But let justice roll down like waters,
and righteousness like an ever-flowing stream.
AMOS 5:24 ESV

The world feels like an unjust place much of the time. People don't always get what they deserve. Maybe you're involved in a legal case and the law has come down on the wrong side of justice. Good people get the shaft while not-so-good ones seem to prosper. Things certainly don't feel just in circumstances like that, do they?

And what about the poor families who work so hard just to put food on the table for their kids. No matter how many hours they put in, the hourly wage from their job falls far short of what they need. It's not fair. They work so hard.

Yes, life is certainly unfair at times. And yet God says that you were created to experience justice. So how does that work?

We won't always see justice in this life, but there's coming a day when all will be made right. And while you're waiting, look for God to surprise you with little reminders that He is your Defender, even now. Don't give up even if you've been wronged. With the blink of an eye, God can make it right again.

I trust You, Lord. Right the wrongs, I pray. Amen.

More Creative Ideas

In the beginning God created the heavens and the earth.
GENESIS 1:1 NIV

Marla was always coming up with ideas for this or that. It seemed she was a never-ending fount of creativity. She could always be counted on at work to put together the winning campaign, so the boss called on her a lot. And at church she was a natural when it came to decorating the fellowship hall for the annual women's conference, which is why the pastor's wife was always open to her plans. Marla seemed to overflow with fun, creative ideas—things others didn't think of.

Maybe you're a creative person too. That's good! You were created in the image of your very creative heavenly Father, after all, and He came up with quite a few clever ideas too. Like giraffes. And butterflies. And honeybees. And to think, all of life got its start when God created the heavens and the earth!

Don't be surprised when that next big idea comes. God might whisper it in your ear even now if you listen closely enough.

I'm so glad I was created in Your image, God.
I love my creativity. Use it for Your glory, I pray. Amen.

More Peace When You're Focused on Him

You keep him in perfect peace whose mind is stayed on you, because he trusts in you.

ISAIAH 26:3 ESV

Crime rates are up. Friends on the opposite side of the political aisle are angry that you don't see things their way. Kids are bickering. The husband isn't happy with something that happened at work. The dog just threw up on the carpet. And the meat you planned to cook for dinner? It's spoiled.

Oh, and you? You're just about to lose it.

When you hit those points—when everything around you is spinning out of control—how do you respond? Do you hide in a closet and scream? Do you yell at the kids, thinking that one outburst will solve all of the problems at once?

God designed you to focus on Him, in good times and bad. It's easier in good times, sure, but you sense His presence even more when you still your heart during tough seasons.

So take a deep breath, sister. Even now—right now, in the middle of the drama—you can be calm, cool, and collected.

Your peace is supernatural, Lord. That's why I depend on it so much! Thanks for giving it when I need it most. Amen.

More Refining

Therefore, since we have these promises, dear friends, let us purify ourselves from everything that contaminates body and spirit, perfecting holiness out of reverence for God.

2 CORINTHIANS 7:1 NIV

Precious metals like gold and silver go through an intense refining process. They're heated to the boiling point and the dross (imperfect portion) falls away, leaving only the precious. The result is pure gold or pure silver, exquisite and valuable. The real deal.

God often puts His kids through the refining process too. Why? He wants you to be the real deal, just like that gold and silver. Right now (shocker!) you're imperfect. It's true. You are holding on to things from the past that you need to release. You have allowed little sins to slip in. That stuff has to go. Don't be surprised if they get squeezed out by life's circumstances. That's often how God works. It's not always pleasant, but in the end all that is left is more precious than any valuable metal.

You were designed by the Lord to be refined. Going through the fire isn't easy, but if the end result is to be more like Him, then it's worth every minute.

Lord, I need Your refiner's fire! Out with the dross! Refine me, I pray. Amen.

More Good and Perfect Gifts

Every good gift and every perfect gift is from above,
coming down from the Father of lights, with whom
there is no variation or shadow due to change.
JAMES 1:17 ESV

All of her life, Kassy's mom would say, "Honey, I just want the best for you."

Kassy did her best not to groan aloud, but she knew what that meant. Mom disagreed with her current choices and wanted something better for her than what she had chosen for herself. (Why did Mom always have to be right?)

God wants "better" for you as well. No matter how many precious gifts life throws your way, His are bigger, better, holier. So don't try to out-do Him! Don't ever think, *I know what's best for myself, so I'll take it from here, God.* Truth is, only He knows what's best, and He's already planning to dish it out. So don't waste your time attempting to outmaneuver your loving heavenly Father. He is, after all, the giver of all good gifts! (And boy, does he want to lavish them on you today!)

You give good gifts, Lord, better than anything I could come up
with for myself. Thank You for showering me with love. Amen.

More Courage

"Have I not commanded you? Be strong and courageous.
Do not be afraid; do not be discouraged, for the LORD
your God will be with you wherever you go."
JOSHUA 1:9 NIV

"Me? Brave?" Trina laughed. "Um, no. I'm the least brave person I know."

"Trina, you need to stop saying that." Her best friend, Ida, clucked her tongue. "You've been through cancer treatment, a house fire, and the loss of your mother, and you still have your faith. I'd say you're one of the bravest women I've ever known."

Trina still wasn't sure. Right now she didn't feel so brave. Her knees were knocking, her hands trembling, and her "want-to" fading.

Maybe you've been there. You need the courage to accomplish something big. Or maybe it's not even big. Maybe it's just a particular task at work you've been dreading. You don't have the courage to tackle it, but guess who does? The same God who raised Jesus from the dead wants to intervene in your situation and give you courage in the moment when you feel your weakest.

You were made for more courage, girl. More and more and more. So square those shoulders. Don't let those wobbly knees worry you. God's got this. And with His hand in yours, you've got it too.

I'm done talking about how cowardly I am, Lord!
I'll speak brave words over my situation today.
With Your help, I've got this. Amen.

More Undefiled Religion

*Religion that is pure and undefiled before God the Father
is this: to visit orphans and widows in their affliction,
and to keep oneself unstained from the world.*

JAMES 1:27 ESV

Carrie considered herself a very religious woman. She rarely missed a Sunday service, gave money to the church on a regular basis, and attended women's Bible study. But sometimes she wondered if her "religion" was nothing but rote. She longed for something deeper, something that connected her to God and to His people.

That fall Carrie started helping out at a women's shelter. There she met women and children who were down on their luck. What started out as a task soon turned into a great joy for Carrie as she shared her faith with many of those she met and watched them turn their situations over to Jesus.

Stepping out of your comfort zone isn't always easy, but it is rewarding. Maybe you need a faith booster. Volunteering to help your local food bank or homeless shelter is a great way to start. Or maybe you can head up the Meals on Wheels program for your community. Regardless, you'll find your faith boosted in no time as you turn your focus outward.

*May my religion be undefiled, Lord! May I be found
caring for the ones who mean so much to You—
the widows, the orphans, and others in need. Amen.*

More Chances to Live Out the Christ Life

Whoever claims to love God yet hates a brother or sister is a liar.
For whoever does not love their brother and sister, whom they
have seen, cannot love God, whom they have not seen.

1 JOHN 4:20 NIV

"Do as I say, not as I do." How many times have you felt like saying that? You want to lead by example but fail miserably at times. (Hey, at least you're not alone! We all fail miserably at times, so you're in good company!)

Aren't you glad God doesn't give up on you even when you're ready to give up on yourself? He gives you chance after chance to live it out, even after the big mess-ups. No, you won't always get it right, but when you do, it feels really good. And it's a lovely reflection of Him for all who are watching.

You'll have plenty of chances ahead to lead by example, so don't spend too much time agonizing over the past. Just keep your eyes on Him and keep moving forward.

I want to be a good example for others, Lord, a light that shines
in the darkness. I confess, I've often messed up and been a
"Don't let this happen to you" example, instead. But I'll keep
forging ahead. Thanks to Your wonderful forgiveness,
I have plenty of chances to get this right. Amen.

More Trust in I Am

God said to Moses, "I AM WHO I AM." And he said,
"Say this to the people of Israel, 'I AM has sent me to you.'"
EXODUS 3:14 ESV

Remember that game you used to play as a kid—the trust game? A group of friends would gather behind you as you were standing. You would fall backward, knowing (or trusting) that they would catch you. Sometimes they would, and sometimes they wouldn't!

You're still playing that game all these years later. How many times have you stumbled and fallen, only to realize that God (the great I Am) was right there, ready to catch you in His arms? Plenty!

You were made to trust Him, even during those seasons when it seems impossible. He has never let you down, and you have no reason to think He'll start now. He's the only trustworthy One. "I Am" means He's ever-present. He is in your situation, even now, ready to help. So place your trust in Him, girl, not in yourself.

Lord, You are the great I Am, the One who is worthy of my praise!
You are present in the very middle of my circumstances. When I
don't know what's happening, You do. I trust You, Holy God! Amen.

More Rejoicing

*"The LORD your God is with you, the Mighty Warrior who saves.
He will take great delight in you; in his love he will no longer
rebuke you, but will rejoice over you with singing."*

ZEPHANIAH 3:17 NIV

What does it mean to rejoice? Evangeline wasn't so sure. Did it mean she had to go around with a fake smile plastered on her face all day to convince nonbelievers that Christians somehow had it better? She still faced difficult things in her life, and faking it didn't seem like the best way to go. People would see right through her if she faked it anyway. She'd never been very good at acting. Nor did she believe God really wanted her to.

As she grew in her faith, Evangeline began to understand that God's version of joy was a lot deeper than feelings. He wasn't asking her to fake, but rather to trust. He wanted her to see that He would carry her when she couldn't carry herself, that He would still perform miracles, usually when she least expected them.

God proved His delight in her in so many surprising ways that she finally found the joy she'd been looking for. It came from His deep, abiding presence.

*Lord, I'm excited to see that You take delight in me!
You rejoice over me with singing, Father.
What a lovely image that is! Amen.*

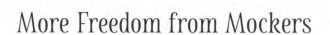

More Freedom from Mockers

*Blessed is the one who does not walk in step
with the wicked or stand in the way that sinners
take or sit in the company of mockers.*

PSALM 1:1 NIV

God has delivered you from many things in your lifetime, hasn't He? But did you know that He wants to deliver you from the hands of mockers? Those people who bite and snap and make fun of you are no fun. And God takes them very seriously. He wants to show you how to free yourself from them while also showing his love to them in the process. (That's not easy, is it? Treating mockers with kindness? What?)

God is also wanting to rid you of any mocking you might be doing. (Let's be honest, we all have a sarcastic, mocking side.) Is there someone—or something—you've been making fun of? If so, it's time to lay that down.

Mocking isn't part of God's plan. He created you for freedom— total and complete freedom in Him. That can only come as you rid yourself of the things that once bound you. So turn your back on mocking once and for all.

*Lord, it hurts to be mocked. And I'm sure I've hurt
others with my sarcastic comments at times. Rid me
of the need to make fun of others, I pray. Amen.*

More Blankets of Love

Whoever would foster love covers over an offense,
but whoever repeats the matter separates close friends.

PROVERBS 17:9 NIV

Love is like a big, cozy blanket. You can toss it over cold, near-impossible situations, and they warm up. It really is the answer to so many of the problems you'll face in this life, especially those difficult relationships.

Is there someone in your life who needs a blanket of love? Perhaps this would be a good day to make a list of all of those in need.

That elderly neighbor, for instance. The checker at the grocery store who always looks so sad. That postal worker who looks so troubled. Maybe you could think of ways to brighten their day.

And while you're at it, why not think big? Why not send a note of encouragement to someone who has played a positive role in your life? He or she might need a boost today.

You were created to blanket people with love. Trust God to show you who, how, and when.

Lord, so many people in my world need more love.
I want to play my part by encouraging them.
Show me who I can bless today, Father. Amen.

More Rest for Your Soul

Take my yoke upon you and learn from me, for I am gentle and humble in heart, and you will find rest for your souls.
MATTHEW 11:29 NIV

We were only meant to carry certain weights. When we pick up burdens that aren't really ours to bear, we're weighing ourselves down unnecessarily. Your friend's marital woes? Sure, you need to care about her, but if you get in the middle of it, you'll have regrets. Your daughter's squabbles with her best friend? It's not yours to fix. That fiasco going on at work? Don't go there, girl!

The only way to find true rest for our souls is to take the yokes that are meant for us, nothing more and nothing less. Pick up too much and you'll sink. Pick up too little and you won't learn how to handle problems as they crop up.

God designed your soul to be at rest. So problems or no problems, you can rest easy in the fact that He's going to take care of you.

Lord, I'm so glad my soul can rest in You. I'll admit I've taken on some burdens that weren't mine to carry. They gave me turmoil, not rest. But You, Lord? You bring peace in the storm and rest when I'm weary. I'm so grateful. Amen.

More Faith

But when you ask, you must believe and not doubt,
because the one who doubts is like a wave of
the sea, blown and tossed by the wind.

JAMES 1:6 NIV

"Do you have faith to believe?"

Marla shook her head. "Not really, if you want the truth. Right now I'm just not feeling it."

She wanted to believe for a godly spouse but kept ending up with guys who were losers. If a great guy actually existed, she hadn't met him yet. And sure she wanted to believe that God would take care of the mess she'd made with her finances, but right now that definitely looked impossible.

Maybe you've walked a mile in Marla's shoes. Things are so out of control that you think they'll never line up. God can take any situation—even a chaotic one—and turn it around if you just believe.

Do you wonder sometimes why God doesn't just do it, whether you believe or not? He's wanting to activate your faith so that you can play a role in the miracle. (How exciting is that?)

So summon your faith. Get ready to watch God move! You were created for more faith, girl!

Lord, I'm ready! I'm so tired of living a faithless life.
Show off, God! Make it big! And include me in the
process as my faith is grown, I pray. Amen.

More Unity

*I appeal to you, brothers and sisters, in the name of our
Lord Jesus Christ, that all of you agree with one another
in what you say and that there be no divisions among you,
but that you be perfectly united in mind and thought.*

1 CORINTHIANS 1:10 NIV

Divisions can be ruthless. Cracks in the surface of a relationship can turn into caverns if the parties involved don't stop them at their root. And there's nothing worse than realizing you're in the middle of a split between friends. Ouch. Talk about painful. (And where do you place your loyalties when friends are divided? What a mess!)

God created His children to be unified. It's not easy, but it's the only way to keep His church working in power. When schisms are created, the body (as a whole) can operate with as much effectiveness. The church grows weak.

The body of Christ was never meant to be weak. Neither were you. So, to the best of your ability, remain unified with those in your local church. It's not always easy, but unity will keep you all strong.

*Lord, thank You for the body of Christ. May we all
seek unity in You today so that power will flow! Amen.*

More Glimpses of Heaven

"He will wipe away every tear from their eyes, and death shall be no more, neither shall there be mourning, nor crying, nor pain anymore, for the former things have passed away."

REVELATION 21:4 ESV

Perhaps you've read stories about people who died, had glimpses of heaven, and then returned. It's remarkable to think that these tiny peeks into the vast unknown have so many similarities.

Heaven is an extraordinary place. If you used your imagination to guess what it would be like, you'd only scratch the surface.

No more pain. No more tears. Spending eternity in worship to the One who makes all things new. Streets of gold. Walls of gemstones. A river flowing from the throne of God. My goodness, it's going to be amazing!

There's only one way to get a true picture of heaven, and that's to assure yourself that you're actually going there someday. You can settle that question today by committing your life to Jesus as Lord and Savior and asking Him to live in your heart. Once that's done, you're on your way to a blissful eternity!

*Lord, I was created to spend eternity with You!
I can't wait for that day. Thank You for giving
me tiny glimpses, even now. Amen.*

More of His Face

"The Lord bless you and keep you; the Lord make his
face shine on you and be gracious to you; the LORD
turn his face toward you and give you peace."
NUMBERS 6:24–26 NIV

In Exodus 30 Moses asked to look upon God's face. God said that was impossible because no one can look on the face of God and live. Why do you suppose that is? The glory of the Lord passed by, and Moses saw just enough of the Lord that His face was radiant.

And yet we cry out to God all the time, "I want to see Your face." Why do we do that?

We were made to see Him face-to-face. And one day we will. When we reach heaven, the Lord—in all His brilliance—will greet us with that glorious face shining on us. We'll spend eternity in His presence, in a never-ending state of joy.

More of His face means more of Him. And more of Him for all eternity? Yes, please!

Lord, I can't wait to see you face-to-face. I'm blessed to spend time
in Your presence now, but there's coming a day, Jesus, when I'll be
in Your presence for all eternity! What a day that will be! Amen.

More Smoothing Things Out

A friend loves at all times, and a brother
is born for a time of adversity.
PROVERBS 17:17 NIV

Let's face it: hanging out with friends is fun—except when it isn't. Sometimes friends get into unnecessary tiffs over the silliest things. Often one will assert herself or feel the need to be right. Sometimes people disagree over politics or even diet plans. We let crazy things divide us.

Here's a great truth: God created you to smooth things out. He doesn't want those tiffs to last forever. In fact, He'd prefer they not happen at all. But when they do, make them short-lived. Be quick to say, "I'm sorry." Be just as quick to say, "Apology accepted." Smooth those ruffled feathers and step back long enough to say, "Can't we all just get along?"

It doesn't matter who was right or wrong. That's often not the point. What matters is that you extend the hand of friendship and exhibit the character of Christ by bringing unity to the situation. You were created for that, after all.

Lord, thank You for the reminder that I can
and should smooth things out. I'll lay down
my pride and do the right thing, Father. Amen.

More Trials to Triumph

Consider it pure joy, my brothers and sisters, whenever you face trials of many kinds, because you know that the testing of your faith produces perseverance. Let perseverance finish its work so that you may be mature and complete, not lacking anything. If any of you lacks wisdom, you should ask God, who gives generously to all without finding fault, and it will be given to you.

JAMES 1:2–5 NIV

Penny wasn't sure why she had so many trials in her life. Some people said it must have been something she'd done—that she had somehow caused herself a life of heartache and pain. She found their words cruel, especially because she'd been a Christian since childhood and had tried, to the best of her ability, to live a godly life.

It didn't seem fair that catastrophe after catastrophe happened, but at the end of each one, Penny was always able to share some sort of testimony of how God had come through for her.

Maybe, like Penny, you've gone from tragedy to triumph. Maybe you've been in the middle of a catastrophic event when the Lord intervened and turned the mess into a message.

God created you to have more "trials to triumph" stories. He doesn't intend for you to be struggling all the time. Remember, you have a very real enemy out there, and he's out to steal, kill, and destroy. You can overcome him, though, when you take authority in the name of Jesus!

Lord, thank You for the many times you've turned my tragedies into triumphs! Amen.

More Angelic Intervention

He will command his angels concerning
you to guard you in all your ways.
Psalm 91:11 NIV

Sally started collecting angels when she was in her teens. Some were porcelain, others were glass. Some were paintings, others were sketches. Her world was filled with angelic beings. By the time she was married, she had a large collection. Looking at them always reminded her of Psalm 91:11, that God will give His angels charge over us. That brought her comfort, particularly during difficult times.

Hebrews 1:14 says that angels are "ministering spirits sent to serve those who will inherit salvation." So if you have committed your life to Christ, the angels serve you. That means they are truly watching over us at all times. Someday when we get to heaven, we may learn about all the times angels protected us from harm even when we weren't aware of their presence.

Have you kept the angels busy? Some people are more adventurous than others! In heaven angels will be our constant companions, as they are now, but we'll actually get to see them up close and personal!

Thank You for sending Your angels to
watch over me, Lord. You care enough to
protect me night and day. I'm so grateful! Amen.

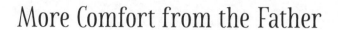

More Comfort from the Father

Even though I walk through the darkest valley, I will fear no evil,
for you are with me; your rod and your staff, they comfort me.

PSALM 23:4 NIV

When you're grieving—when the pain is so fresh you're doubled over from the sheer gravity of the loss—you think you'll never smile again. Life will never be worthy of living. You'll never draw another breath without aching for the one you've lost. It seems impossible that the sun might continue to rise in breathtaking colors each morning and set again at night. How could it, when your world has been so violently rocked?

During this earth-shattering season, God's presence can be just as real as ever. In fact, He longs so deeply for you to be comforted that He draws close, His rod and staff easing you in His direction.

God hasn't forgotten about you. He sees the pain. He knows the agony. He's right here, arms extended, saying, "Come to Me for comfort. I love you, My precious child, and I truly care."

Lord, sometimes the ache is so real that I wonder if I can
go on. During these seasons I need You more than ever.
Thank You for meeting me in my darkest valley. I'm not
afraid, as long as I know You're right here. Amen.

More Sufficiency

My God will meet all your needs according
to the riches of his glory in Christ Jesus.
PHILIPPIANS 4:19 NIV

God longs for His kids to have sufficiency in all things at all times. He's not keen on you going without food, lodging, transportation, or anything else, for that matter. Why? Because He loves you. And He has work for you to do. It's harder to get things done when you're hungry, homeless, and lacking transportation. You lose your ability to focus when your tummy is rumbling!

When your needs are met, you can thrive. When you're not hyper-focused on your lack, your mind is freed up to do the things that matter. So God's promise to provide is a practical one, as well as one rooted in love.

Today, make a list of all the ways God has proven Himself faithful as a provider. That job? Your home? The groceries in your pantry? Has He not provided all those things and more? Why not offer a word of thanks to the Almighty for caring so deeply that your needs are met.

I get it, Lord! I was made for more of Your provision.
How grateful I am for Your sufficiency! Amen.

More Unsearchable Things

*"Call to me and I will answer you and tell you great
and unsearchable things you do not know."*

JEREMIAH 33:3 NIV

McKinsey wasn't sure who to go to with the big questions: Why do bad things happen to good people? Why does God allow sickness and pain in this life? Why is Jesus the only way to heaven? She was filled with questions like these and eventually found a godly friend who helped her search out answers in the Bible.

Maybe you're struggling to find answers to life's deeper questions too. You're wondering some of the same things McKinsey is. Search the Word of God and you'll find verse after verse to shed light on most of your questions, of course, but don't forget to go directly to the Lord.

God isn't afraid of your tough questions during your prayer times. He doesn't get offended or upset if you say, "I don't get it, Lord. Why did You allow this (or that) to happen?" He's gentle enough to whisper His responses in your ear, all the while bringing comfort to your heart.

The Lord made you to call on Him. He longs to tell you great and unsearchable things. But first you have to ask.

What will you ask Him today?

Lord, today I'll start with this question:

_____ *(fill in the blank).*

More Effective Prayers

*"Pray then like this: Our Father in heaven,
hallowed be your name."*

<small>MATTHEW 6:9 ESV</small>

Cathy knew she made a mistake by opening her door to a salesman.

"This handy-dandy multipurpose cleaner will leave all your surfaces bright and shiny!" He held up a bottle of magic liquid and smiled. "Just spray it on your dirtiest spots, and you'll see instantaneous results!"

She rather doubted it but ended up buying a bottle just to get rid of the man.

Maybe you've purchased a product that promised to be more effective than all others. Perhaps you were disappointed with the results.

Here's a fun fact: Your prayers can be more effective than any magic potion or cleansing powder. They can do things you never dreamed they could do! Miracles can happen when you pray. And girl, you were made to believe that! God created you to believe that your prayers could move mountains.

So, what's holding you back? Ready, set, pray!

Father, I'm so grateful my prayers are effective. They're not like that product I bought—all hype. You'll really work on my circumstances when I pray. How grateful I am! Amen.

More Willing to Work

Whatever you do, work at it with all your heart,
as working for the Lord, not for human masters.
COLOSSIANS 3:23 NIV

Remember the old Disney movie *Snow White*? She stumbles into the world of the seven dwarves, who seem to be nothing short of workaholics. Every day they head off to work, singing a merry tune to prepare them for the day ahead.

Do you head off to work each morning with a song on your heart too? The same joy that propelled the dwarves to work should drive you to the tasks at hand too.

Not feeling it? No worries! Just turn on a worship song and sing your heart out as you drive, drive, drive to the office. "Hi-ho! Hi-ho! Your heart is changing so! The more you worship, the better you feel, hi-ho, hi-ho!"

You were created to work. And your willingness to dive right in is important. God isn't looking for slouches! Only the finest for the work at hand! So, get to it. Hi-ho, girl!

Lord, I don't always approach my work with a hi-ho
attitude, but here I go! Thank You for giving me
the desire to work hard, Father. Amen.

More Passion for Children

Jesus said, "Let the little children come to me, and do not hinder
them, for the kingdom of heaven belongs to such as these."

MATTHEW 19:14 NIV

How do you feel about children? Oh, not the whole, "Should I become a mother?" thing, but children in general. Do you feel drawn to them? Do you enjoy working with them—at church, in the neighborhood, or across the board?

Children are the closest thing to heaven this life offers. Their innocent little faces. Those impish smiles. Those cute little bangs. Their silly sing-songy ways. Oh, how they radiate all that is good and right with the world.

You were created to have more passion for children—not just those you can see with your eyes, but even children on other continents. What does that look like? Maybe it looks like you donating funds to a missionary so that he or she can share the Gospel in a third world country. Maybe it means giving a monthly donation to an organization that supports children across the globe. Perhaps it looks like volunteering in your church's nursery.

Whatever it looks like to you, dive right in! Those little ones will change your life for the better.

Point me in the direction of a child
whose life I can enrich, Lord. Amen.

More Submission

Trust in the LORD with all your heart and lean not on your own understanding; in all your ways submit to him, and he will make your paths straight.

PROVERBS 3:5–6 NIV

"More of You, less of me." Nina spoke the words aloud. More of the Lord meant more time submitting to His will, His way. No longer could she tackle her problems in the usual way; now she had to wait on Him for the perfect solution.

If you're like Nina, you're not a fan of waiting on God. And submitting to His perfect will during the waiting? That seems nonsensical at times. And yet that's what He requires.

Why? Because the Lord wants to make sure you fully trust Him. When He's convinced you're looking to Him and not yourself, He's free to move.

Submission isn't really an ugly word. To submit just means you bow to God's authority. And isn't that the ultimate goal, really—for His authority to reign?

Lord, I submit to Your authority, even while I'm waiting for the answers I seek. I know I can trust You because of Your deep love for me, Father. So I'm here, heart and head bowed, while I wait. Amen.

More Emotional Healing

In his kindness God called you to share in his eternal glory by means of Christ Jesus. So after you have suffered a little while, he will restore, support, and strengthen you, and he will place you on a firm foundation.

1 PETER 5:10 NLT

"You will not suffer forever."

How do you feel when you read those words? Do you find them difficult to believe, or do they bring great hope?

God never intended for your emotional suffering to last a lifetime. All along He had a plan for the healing of your heart and mind. In His kindness, this verse says, He called you to share in His glory. That kindness brings what you need the most: restoration, support for your soul, strength as only He can give, and ultimately a firm foundation to walk on after the crisis has passed.

You were created for emotional healing, not a lifetime of endless pain. Begin to lift your heart and your eyes, even now. No matter how deep the waters, no matter how intense the pain, God is right there, extending a hand of kindness. Even now He longs to make you whole.

Lord, I've been through so much pain in my life. Sometimes it seems unfair, when I compare my journey to others. But You, Father, have offered healing when I need it most. Touch my heart, I pray. Amen.

More of the Spirit, Less of the Flesh

*"Watch and pray that you may not enter into temptation.
The spirit indeed is willing, but the flesh is weak."*

MATTHEW 26:41 NIV

"The Spirit is willing, but the flesh is weak."

Maybe you've heard those words and wondered what they meant.

When you try (in your own strength) to complete a task, the chances of things working out well are pretty slim. Even on your best day you're still not Wonder Woman. But when you add God to the equation, well, that changes everything!

The Spirit of God brings supernatural power from on high to accomplish things you could only dream of accomplishing on your own. That's why it's important to realize you were never meant to operate in your own strength alone. You were created for more of His Spirit and less of your flesh.

Lord, I try so hard! I'm a regular worker bee. I buzz, buzz, buzz along, doing all I can in my flesh, and then I wonder why things don't work out. I've left out a key ingredient! Your Spirit is what I need to energize, bring power, and give me the direction I need. I invite You today, Holy Spirit, to enter my situation. Amen.

More Things

"But seek first the kingdom of God and his righteousness, and all these things will be added to you."

MATTHEW 6:33 ESV

We're promised in scripture that if we seek God's kingdom first and foremost, then "all these things" will be added to us.

All *what* things? The things we're praying for? The things on our wish list? What things will be added to us?

God wants to provide all we need physically—our daily provisions, such as food, shelter, and clothing—but He also longs to give us things to build us up from the inside-out, things like grace, peace, joy, kindness, self-control, and so on. These are essential building blocks.

If you're lacking those things, why not do what this scripture suggests—seek His kingdom first? Oh, I know, it makes no sense to you. Put Him first and that somehow meets *your* needs?

Yes. Put Him first and He makes sure every need is met. It's that simple—and that complicated.

All things are promised to you, girl, if you can just get those priorities straight.

> *Lord, I get it! I'll put You first and You'll make sure*
> *I'm covered. Today I choose to do just that. Amen.*

More Assurance of His Promises

"If you ask me anything in my name, I will do it."
JOHN 14:14 ESV

"Do you promise?" Drenda crossed her arms at her chest as she looked her husband's way. "You promise to fix the broken fence this coming weekend?"

"I do!" He put his hand up as if giving a Boy Scout's pledge. "I'll do it on Saturday."

But Saturday came and he got busy doing something else entirely. The fence continued to rot and the dog continued to escape, as always. It was all Drenda could do not to get angry. Instead, she dragged the doghouse in front of the busted fence and made a makeshift wall so the pooch couldn't get out. It worked—for a while.

Maybe you're like Drenda, tired of broken promises. Well, here's some good news: God will never break His promises to you. His promises are "Yes!" and "Amen!" (2 Corinthians 1:20).

No matter how many broken promises you've faced in life, you can rest assured the Lord of heaven and earth won't let you down. Never ever.

Lord, I can trust You. If you say it, You'll do it!
That brings such assurance! I was created to be
sure of You, Father. Oh, how grateful I am! Amen.

More Focused on Others

*Do nothing from selfish ambition or conceit, but in
humility count others more significant than yourselves.*
PHILIPPIANS 2:3 ESV

Mary Anne couldn't help it that she was born an only child. Was it her fault her parents had spoiled her rotten and given her everything she ever wanted? Sure, she turned out a little demanding. But was that really her fault? She'd been conditioned from childhood to think she was the center of the universe, after all.

Maybe you've known a few Mary Annes in your life. They sit enthroned on high, far above the meager servants below. They always get what they want when they want it. And they don't often care who they have to step on to get it.

God didn't create you to be a queen, princess. Seriously. He created you to think more of others than yourself. If anyone is going to be elevated in your story, let it be those around you—the school lunch lady, for example. The bus driver. The postal worker. The doctor who works around the clock.

It's not all about you. It never was. Those words might sting, but they will also bring you life.

*Lord, I'm sorry for the times I've made everything about me.
I'll be more outward focused from now on. Amen.*

More Escapes

There hath no temptation taken you but such as is common to man: but God is faithful, who will not suffer you to be tempted above that ye are able; but will with the temptation also make a way to escape, that ye may be able to bear it.

1 CORINTHIANS 10:13 KJV

Olivia lifted her pencil from the maze and studied it carefully. If she took this route right here—no, that wouldn't work. She ended up at a dead end once again. What about this route? She rested her pencil tip on the page and drew the line, but it too ended at a dead end.

Maybe you've been there. You've tried to maneuver your way through life's situations and found yourself at dead end after dead end. No matter what you tried, you couldn't escape. After a while you felt trapped.

God never intended for you to feel trapped! He's faithful. He won't let you be tempted above what you're able. He always provides a way of escape—from that abusive relationship. From financial woes. From fear. From anger. From everything that has haunted and plagued you from childhood.

You weren't meant to carry it always. Eyes wide open! The escape hatch is just ahead. You'll find it as long as you keep your eyes on Him.

Lord, my eyes are fixed on You. I don't want to miss the big escape! You're about to take me from pain to joy, Father, and I'm so grateful! Amen.

The "More" Lifestyle

God is able to bless you abundantly, so that in all things at all times, having all that you need, you will abound in every good work.

2 CORINTHIANS 9:8 NIV

Have you figured it out, sweet girl? God adores you. He thinks you're the cat's meow. And He has many wonderful things planned for you. You have more places to go, people to see, and things to do. There's more love, more hope, more joy, and more opportunity to experience His goodness as you move forward from here.

It's time to adopt a "more" lifestyle. Live with a sense of expectation. See yourself as a conqueror! Enjoy the possibilities of what's coming around the bend. And remember, God's love for you isn't just for a day; it's for all eternity. (Can you even imagine what "more" will look like in heaven?)

Lord, thank You for creating me for more! It's because of Your great love that I've received so many blessings along life's journey. And I know there's more coming, not just here, but in heaven. Oh, how I long for that day, Father, when we'll see each other face-to-face! Amen.